Bringing Out Baby

2nd Edition

Bringing Out Baby

2nd Edition

Places to take Babies and Toddlers

Seattle, the Eastside and South Snohomish County

Rebecca Johnston

JOHNSTON
ASSOCIATES
INTERNATIONAL

P.O. BOX 313
MEDINA, WASHINGTON 98039
(425) 454-7333 • FAX (425) 462-1335
ONLINE ADDRESS: jasibooks@aol.com

Bringing Out Baby: Places to take Babies and Toddlers
Seattle, the Eastside and South Snohomish County, 2nd Edition
© 2006 by Rebecca Johnston

P.O. Box 313
Medina, Washington 98039
(425)454-7333; fax: (425)462-1335
e-mail: jasibooks@aol.com
Web site: www.jasibooks.com

ISBN 1-881409-32-5
Cover and book design: Mike Jaynes
Production, typesetting, and layout: Mike Jaynes

Printed in the United States of America

Library of Congress Cataloging-in-Publication Data

Johnston, Rebecca, 1970-
  Bringing out baby : places to take babies and toddlers : Seattle, the
Eastside, and South Snohomish County / Rebecca Johnston. -- 2nd ed.
      p. cm.
  Originally published: Bringing out baby : Seattle & the Eastside : places to
take babies & toddlers / Julia Rader Detering. c1999.
  Includes bibliographical references and index.
  ISBN 1-881409-32-5 (pbk.)
  1. Seattle Region (Wash.)--Guidebooks. 2. Family recreation--Washington
(State)--Seattle Region--Guidebooks. 3. Mothers--Travel--Washington
(State)--Seattle Region--Guidebooks. 4. Infants--Travel--Washington
(State)--Seattle Region--Guidebooks. 5. Toddlers--Travel--Washington
(State)--Seattle Region--Guidebooks. I. Detering, Julia Rader, 1963- Bringing
out baby. II. Title.
  F899.S43J655 2006
  917.97'7720444--dc22
                                        2006029510

Acknowledgements

My first thanks must go to Julia Rader Detering, the original author of Bringing Out Baby. This book helped me get through the transition from full-time career woman to stay-at-home mom. Without Julia's hard work and research to develop the first edition, I never would have been inspired or motivated to revise the second.

I must also thank my mother-in-law, Priscilla Johnston, publisher of the first edition, who encouraged me to take on this project. She provided her expertise and support, which proved invaluable, especially on the days where my son wouldn't nap and I couldn't get anything accomplished.

There are multiple locations listed in this book that I wouldn't have found without the help of two dear friends, Amy Wright and Kristi Jenkins. They had a nine-month jump on me in being at home with their babies. They introduced me to their mom friends and graciously shared with me activities and places they had found that were fun for their children.

Mike Jaynes, my book designer, also played a key role in the process of putting this book together. Without him, you wouldn't be reading this book.

Finally, I cannot fail to acknowledge how grateful I am to my husband, Mac, for navigating directions, driving around with me on weekends, and sitting in the car with our sleeping baby boy while I visited parks and facilities. He is so patient! And, of course, were it not for my son, Benjamin, none of this would have happened at all.

Contents

CHAPTER THREE
Shopping

Introduction

My son just turned one as I began the revision of this book. It was the perfect time to reflect on the activities that we enjoyed early on and to think about how I was going to keep him entertained—and myself sane—as he enters his toddler years.

Benjamin was born in April, an unpredictable time of year when it comes to weather in the Seattle area. One day it's 70 degrees and the next it's raining. I've found it's important to have a variety of choices for things to do, depending on what is in store for the day's forecast.

As a new mother, I was lucky to have several friends who had also recently had a baby. We spent quite a bit of time together during my maternity leave, and they shared with me many of the great ways to stay connected with the outside world.

At first, you may think that you never want to leave the comforts of home, but, trust me, you'll end up with severe cabin fever if you succumb to these thoughts for long.

I was home with my son for three months, and my husband stayed home for a month following my return to work. There were outings to parks, the zoo, and restaurants as we enjoyed our new roles as parents. Both my husband and I were back at work by the time our son was four months old. We relished our time in the evenings and on weekends with him, and we continually looked for new things to do. The first edition of *Bringing Out Baby*, published by my mother-in-law, really helped us be creative.

When he was nine months old, I decided that being at home was the best thing for my son and our family. Julia Rader Detering, the original author of *Bringing out Baby*, had declined to do a new edition. She was headed back to work, just as I was leaving the workplace. It was at this point that I really started to take a look at *Bringing Out Baby* and offered to improve on the great content the book already had.

In this edition, you'll find updated information for prior entries, along with new activities and places to go with your infant and/or toddler. You'll notice the format is updated to make the book easier to use. I've also expanded the area covered by the book to include South Snohomish County.

How to Use this Book

This book will lead you to a wealth of interesting places and stimulating activities for children under three. Because the book contains such a broad range of information, it is difficult to neatly categorize everything. However, the information has been grouped into three general chapters: one for inside activities, one for outside activities, and one for shopping areas.

Chapter One: Bringing Out Baby
Creepers, Crawlers & Toddlers – INSIDE

This chapter lists places where you can take your newborn or toddler for indoor activities. Included are the names, phone numbers, and descriptions of support groups, post-partum exercise programs, and infant massage classes that are appropriate for the first months of a newborn's life.

After your baby begins to move about, his or her interests expand and your little one is ready for a new set of activities. This chapter also includes those activities—places that are appropriate for a baby whose world has broadened because of his or her growing mobility and continued developmental advancement.

At the beginning of chapter one is a section titled Multiple

Locations. This section includes those organizations, both public and private, that offer the same type of program at multiple locations. Libraries with storytime for toddlers, swim classes for infants and Kindermusik classes fall into this category. The activity is described, and then all locations are listed.

After the Multiple Locations, the chapter has been divided into geographic areas. Indoor sites are listed alphabetically within each neighborhood.

Chapter Two: Bringing out Baby
Creepers, Crawlers & Toddlers – OUTSIDE

This chapter describes parks and playgrounds that are suitable for youngsters under three years old. The descriptions are organized by neighborhood. Parks that are unkempt or are mostly used by older children are not included in this book. Smaller parks that have a limited play area or limited equipment have been included to benefit parents who live nearby and need a place to stroll. Also, this chapter includes parks without any play equipment because a baby who is not yet crawling does not need much of a playground, if any, but can still benefit from an outing to the park.

Seattle, the Eastside and South Snohomish County have done a wonderful job of preserving land designated for recreation. Funds are allocated for the upkeep of parks and many playgrounds are being refurbished. Beaches are wonderful places to visit on warm days and abound near the various bodies of water that surround the Seattle area.

Chapter Three: Shopping Areas

A third chapter, Bringing Out Baby - Shopping, will help you find grocery stores, malls and shopping centers that are child-friendly and offer some stimulation for your child.

Shopping malls provide a great place to get out of the house and stay out of the rain or beat the heat on a hot day. Major malls are outlined with the names of stores that carry children's apparel, toys and child-friendly restaurants. This chapter also lists the location of nursing and diaper changing areas in each shopping center.

Information Blocks

In the listings, information blocks at the beginning provide a quick summary of what a site has to offer.

Access: If a parking lot or street parking is readily available, and if the site itself can be negotiated with a child in a stroller, it will be noted here. To be "accessible," strollers must be able to roll up to the play equipment for outdoor activities. For indoor activities, the stroller must be able to roll up to the point of destination.

Hours and fees: For museums, zoos, and centers, the hours of operations are listed. Admission fees are listed when they remain relatively constant. Class fees tend to vary and change often, so you will not see this information listed as frequently. Call the facility for current information about classes offered and fees.

Classes: Entries for indoor activities list classes available for children under three. Because classes change frequently, it is best to call and inquire about what is currently being offered.

Weekend/evening hours: If weekend or evening hours are offered for indoor activities, that will be noted. This listing can serve as a quick reference for working parents looking for indoor activities that have classes or playrooms available in the evenings or weekends. If no classes are offered on the weekends or evenings, it will be noted.

Features: Facilities or services, such as restrooms, changing tables, and food or drink availability, are listed here. These are features that are appropriate for a child and will make your visit easier.

A large park with quiet, semiprivate nooks meets the requirement for nursing privacy. Indoor activities that cater to new mothers are designed to put a nursing mother at ease, and in these places privacy may not be necessary.

When a location or activity does not have a significant feature that you may want, such as a restroom, the entry for that location or activity will note that in italics at the end of the information block.

Quick Reference Guide

A quick reference guide at the end of the book provides a list activities and parks by neighborhood.

I hope that through this book you will discover activities for your child that you never realized were available. My message to you is this: Get out of the house, and take that precious new life with you. You will both be enriched by the experience.

CHAPTER ONE
Bringing Out Baby
Creepers, Crawlers & Toddlers
INSIDE

The period when your infant is immobile is precious indeed. I call it the "portable period" because there are some activities that are easier to do with an infant than with a highly active toddler.

Many parents of young children told me to dine out while my infant was very young because taking him to restaurants later would present more of a challenge. Now that I have a toddler who doesn't want to sit still for more than a five-minute stretch, I completely understand that advice.

While dining out with an infant can be an enjoyable way  to spend time outside your house, there are many other activities available for infants younger than six months. You are not relegated solely to going out to eat if you'd like to spend time outside your house with your young infant.

When I began revising this book, my son was older than six months, so I researched activities for the young infant age group by observing the class, interviewing the instructor or coordinator, or confirming the information contained in the first edition. In many cases I was able to visit the location of each program to gain a better idea of the parking, restrooms and food availability.

Programs and classes exist that are especially designed for these babies. The exercise classes may be called "post-partum" aerobics. Massage classes are designed for babies that lie still. The support groups begin when your baby is a newborn and continue as your baby ages.

Again, I strongly recommend getting out of the house with your young infant. It is very easy to become a shut-in after your child is born. Anyone with a new baby knows that you don't give birth and become your old self immediately. Getting out of the house will encourage you to get yourself together, build back your self-esteem and increase your energy.

After your child becomes mobile, activities outside the home become even more essential. As soon as your baby starts sitting up, he or she is eager to experience new sensations, and exploring new places together can be stimulating for both of you. For inclement weather, numerous indoor activities and places are available. Most indoor activities are ideal for a baby who can walk, although less mobile infants can be entertained as well. Community centers, family support centers, and private enterprises offer many classes, play areas, and activities for babies of all ages.

At community centers, classes follow a quarterly schedule; call for schedules and fees, as you will need to register before classes begin. Classes at private facilities often follow a quarterly schedule also. However, some other types of facilities offer ongoing registration. The cost of classes varies widely. At community centers they usually average under $10 per session and can be as little as $3 per session. Activities at commercial locations most often are more expensive, averaging $15 per class. Most indoor activities offer a free preview of the class; call to inquire if such an option is available.

Probably the most popular recreations are the open gyms and indoor playgrounds located at various community centers. They are available to children under five years old. Be aware that these facilities tend to fill up with running toddlers and therefore can be hazardous for smaller infants. Because they are inexpensive, costing between $2 and $3 per child, they are excellent places to take several children. The hours these facilities are open vary widely and can change from quarter to quarter so you must always check beforehand.

Indoor playgrounds are wonderful places for young crawlers and walkers to burn off energy and meet other youngsters. These are excellent spots to follow the advice of The American Academy of Pediatrics: "The best way for your child to learn how to behave around other people is to be given plenty of trial runs."

Multiple Locations

The following activities have branches throughout King and Snohomish Counties. Call for specific information.

AMC THEATER REEL MOMS

www.moviewatcher.com/reelmoms

(206) 622-2434

1501 7th Avenue, Seattle, Meridian 16

(425) 921-2985

18733 33rd Avenue W., Lynnwood, Alderwood Mall 16

Hours and fees: Every Tuesday 11 a.m., matinee price for parent, free for baby

Access: Parking available; stroller access and stroller check, changing table

AMC's Reel Moms program (also open to Dads) shows first run movies in a theater that is geared exclusively for parents and their children under age two. The theater keeps the lights low and reduces the sound. If you need to get out of the house but aren't feeling particularly energetic, this activity is right for you. I attended when my son was three months old and he slept the entire time. There were also toddlers who were playing rather than watching the movie. The best part of the Reel Mom's movie program is that if your child cries, no one turns around to give you a dirty look!

BABY BOOT CAMP

(425) 281-1635 in Redmond or **www.babybootcamp.com** for other locations

Hours and fees: Call for class times and fees

Access: Varies by location, but expect parking and stroller access

Classes: Baby Boot Camp (Moms and babies 6–8 weeks and up)

Features: Vary by location

Baby Boot Camp is a great way to meet other new mothers and to get back in shape at the same time. A 75-minute class focuses on strength training drills combined with cardiovascular intervals. Classes are held outdoors and babies in strollers are an integral part of the workout. All instructors are Certified Fitness Professionals. This is a fantastic way to get some exercise while spending time with your baby.

COOPERATIVE PRESCHOOLS

Cooperative preschools provide a popular venue for you and your baby to interact with other parents and babies. Most community colleges offer some type of cooperative preschool in your area. I recommend these preschools for most people because many of my friends have enjoyed participating in them.

These preschools begin with babies as young as three months old and can continue with the same group of children until they reach age five. They are called a cooperative because the parents participate by cleaning up, providing a snack, and fundraising. During each two-hour class, early childhood education specialists lead discussions about child rearing, and time is provided for parents and children to socialize. Singing, stories and supervised playtime are a part of the meetings.

As babies grow older, mothers can trade time, leaving during the class while their child stays with the remaining parents. The cost of these preschools is much less than a daycare center, but can be more expensive than a class at a community center. These cooperatives fill up quickly so contact them to get on a waiting list as soon as you think you might be interested in them.

The following list of phone numbers will help you find a cooperative preschool near you. If there is more than one city or neighborhood served by a college, only the name of the city or neighborhood is listed.

Bellevue Community College
(425) 641-2366
Bellevue, North Bend, Carnation, Issaquah, May Valley, Preston, Mercer Island

Edmonds Community College
(425) 640-1665
Edmonds, Mill Creek, Mountlake Terrace

Lake Forest Park Cooperative Preschool
(425) 486-3466
6124 NE 181st Street, Kenmore

Lake Washington Technical College
(425) 739-8100
Redmond, Kirkland

North City Parent Cooperative
(206) 362-4069
2545 NE 200th Street, Seattle

North Seattle Community College
(206) 527-3783
Ballard, Green Lake, Loyal Heights, Fremont, Wallingford

Phinney Neighborhood Preschool Cooperative
(206) 706-2963
North Seattle

Seattle Central Community College
(206) 587-6938
Queen Anne, Beacon Hill, Madison Park, Capitol Hill, Madrona, Magnolia, Lakewood

Shoreline Cooperative Preschool
(206) 362-3257
2545 NE 200th Street, Seattle

South Seattle Community College
(206) 938–2278
Lincoln Park, Alki, Arbor Heights, High Point, Vashon

Woodinville Family Preschool
(425) 481-9707
23713 49th Avenue SE, Bothell

GYMBOREE

www.gymboree.com

Hours: Vary depending on the class taken

Fees: $35 lifetime registration fee, $196 for 12-week Play or Music Class, $345 for 24-week Play or Music Class; additional classes or drop-in punch card available for a discounted fee. If you have more than one child enrolled, you'll receive 10% off each additional child.

Access: Lot and/or street access depending on location; stroller access

Weekend/evening hours: Yes

Classes: Level 1 (0-6 months), Level 2 (6-10 months), Level 3 (10-16 months), Level 4 (16-22 months), Level 5 (22-28 months), Level 6 (28-36 months). There are several classes to choose from in each level, including the core Gymboree class, Music, Mommy & Baby Fitness, Yoga, Family Fitness and more.

Gymboree offers developmental play and exercise for babies and toddlers. Classes are divided into age groups that focus on the baby's developmental stage, with the age range in each class increasing as the child grows. An instructor leads parents and babies in using the equipment provided.

At the beginning of the class the teacher explains the focus of the day. For example, on the day we went the focus was on the concepts of fast and slow. The teacher advises parents how to use apparatuses such as a large wedge to demonstrate particular concepts to the child. After this, parents spend most of the time playing with their babies, then the group gathers together for activities such as singing, playing on a large colorful parachute, and blowing bubbles.

These classes may be a little pricey, but babies seem to enjoy them. Before you commit to paying for a class, you can sign up online for a free trial.

Call or check online for times when your child's age group meets.

2622 NW Market Street, Ballard
  (206) 783-3741

735 NW Gilman Boulevard, Suite E,
  Issaquah
  (425) 392-8438

3225 Alderwood Mall Boulevard, Suite G, Lynnwood
  (425) 775-4782

164th Ave NE #I133, Redmond
  (425) 702-8811

7400 Sandpoint Way NE, Suite 105, Sandpoint
  (206) 522-2045

KINDERMUSIK

1–800–628–5687 or **www.kindermusik.com**
  for a location near you

Hours: Vary depending on the class taken

Fees: Vary depending on the class taken and location

Access: Varies depending on instructor's location

Weekend/evening hours: Yes

Kindermusik International has developed a curriculum to introduce youngsters to the world of music. For forty-five minutes, once a week, both parent and child participate in singing, musical instrument exploration and movement.

These structured classes, developed by early childhood education and music specialists, are designed to be fun in addition to being educational. Freelance instructors are trained by Kindermusik International and hold classes in their homes. Kindermusik Village classes are for newborns to age 18 months. Kindermusik Our Time classes are for ages 18 months to 36 months. Kindermusik also offers Sign & Sing, a sign language course for ages 6 months to 3 years, and their newest class, Kindermusik Family Time is geared for families with multiple children, from newborns to age 7. Most locations will offer a free trial class before you commit to signing up.

LA LECHE LEAGUE

(206) 522–1336 Seattle; (425) 303-0311 Snohomish County

www.lalecheleague.org

Hours and fees: Call for class times and fees

Access: Parking available; stroller access varies

Classes: Meet once a month

Features: Restrooms, changing table availability varies, food and drink availability varies, nursing privacy

La Leche League was founded in 1956 by women who had overcome obstacles associated with breastfeeding. It now serves as a support group and advisor for women who are breastfeeding their babies. The meeting I attended was at the Fremont Baptist Church and was held in the evening. About twenty women with their babies sat in a large circle and exchanged thoughts, concerns and questions about breastfeeding.

The La Leche League leader serves as a facilitator of the meeting and addresses questions asked by the nursing mothers. You do not have to be a mother of a newborn to join the meetings. My baby was four months old when I attended because I was concerned about nursing him to sleep. A friend's child was eighteen months old when she wanted to learn about weaning. There were babies of all ages at the meeting, and all sorts of issues were discussed. The La Leche League leader in your area will also help individually with any nursing problem or concern. It's important to recognize that the La Leche League is a staunch supporter of breastfeeding.

THE LITTLE GYM

www.thelittlegym.com

Hours and fees: Call for times and fees of classes

Classes: Bugs (4–10 months), Birds (10–19 months), Beasts (19 months–2 1/2 years)

Weekend/evening hours: Yes

Access: Parking; stroller access

Features: Play equipment for tots (see below), restrooms, changing table

No food or drink available, no nursing privacy

These loosely structured classes give toddlers and infants a chance to run, crawl, climb and bounce on colorful pieces of

equipment. Classes consist of singing and group movement, and also allow free time to explore the equipment. An instructor is on hand to assist parents in teaching their child various methods of using the apparatus. After free play, everyone gathers around the large multicolored parachute for singing and play. The class ends with a good-bye song. These gyms are very stimulating for babies.

1800 130th Avenue NE, Bellevue
(425) 885-3866

690 NW Gilman Blvd., Issaquah
(425)837-1414

6748 NE 181st Street, Kenmore
(425) 481-5889

7777 15th Avenue NE, Seattle
(206) 524-2623

PROGRAM FOR EARLY PARENT SUPPORT (PEPS)

(206) 547–8570

www.pepsgroup.org

Locations vary.

Hours and fees: Call for class times; $125 for one parent, $175 for two parents – a $25 deposit must be paid to be placed in a group. Scholarships are available upon request.

Classes: Newborn Program

Access: Parking available, stroller access varies

Features: Vary depending on location. Restrooms, changing table/area, nursing privacy and a snack can be expected

PEPS provides new parents with support and information through their New Parents program. Groups are organized ac-

cording to your child's birth month and geographic location, so that you are placed with other parents going through the same experiences you are. Usually, there are eight to twelve new mothers/fathers and a volunteer facilitator, often a previous PEPS participant, and you meet for two hours once a week. Gener-

ally, everyone lives in the same neighborhood, so the meetings rotate from home to home. During the first hour the leader facilitates a discussion. The second hour is for free talk, singing to the babies, and snacks for the adults. The discussions are informal, but also informative. Often first-time parents have no idea what normal behavior and emotions are for infant, mother, or father. It is helpful to hear how other parents deal with colic, sleeping, and nursing and eventually weaning, feeding and napping.

Many Community Centers also host PEPS groups, and there are free PEPS Parent/Child Activity Time located at family support centers throughout Seattle and South Snohomish County. These meetings are available to parents with children under three and are perfect for those with more than one child.

PUBLIC LIBRARIES

Some libraries offer Toddler Storytime, Rock and Read, or Mother Goose Storytime—different names for storytime geared toward children under two. For half an hour, a children's librarian or local volunteer reads stories aloud, and arts and crafts activities are sometimes offered. Some classes are split between walkers and non-walkers.

Always phone first for times and availability, as many story times change seasonally or are only offered during certain times of the year. Many of the public libraries have a children's books section that not only has books available for you to read to your child but also has toys and puzzles set out to occupy youngsters.

Ballard Branch–Toddler Storytime
    (206) 684–4089
    5711 NW 24th Avenue

Bellevue Regional Library–Toddler Time
    (425) 450–1775
    1111 N 110th Avenue

Bothell Regional Library-Mother Goose on the Loose
    and Toddler Storytime
    (425) 486-7811
    18215 98th Avenue NE

Edmonds Library–Infant and Toddler Storytime
    (425) 771-1933
    650 Main Street

Green Lake Branch–Toddler Storytime
    (206) 684–7547
    7364 E Green Lake Drive North

Holly Park Branch–Toddler Storytime
    (206) 386–1905
    6748 S 35th Avenue

Issaquah Library–Mother Goose Storytime and Toddler Time
(425) 392–5430
120 E Sunset Way

Kenmore Library-Morning Storytime
(425) 486-8747
18138 73rd NE

Kirkland Public Library–Toddler Time
(425) 822–245
308 Kirkland Avenue

Lake City Branch–Rock and Read
(206) 684–7518
12501 NE 28th Avenue

Lake Hills Library–Mother Goose Storytime and Toddler Time
(425) 747–3350
15228 Lake Hills Boulevard

Lynnwood Library-Baby and Me Storytime and Toddler Storytime
(425) 778-2148
19200 44th Avenue West

Mill Creek Library-Baby Ready Readers and
Toddler/Preschool Ready Readers
(425) 337-4822
15429 Bothell-Everett Highway

Montlake Branch–Toddler Storytime
(206) 684–4720
2300 E 24th Avenue

Mountlake Terrace Library-Storytime
(425) 776-8722
23300 58th Avenue West

Newport Way Library–Mother Goose Storytime and Toddler Time
(425) 747–2390
14250 SE Newport Way

Northeast Branch–Toddler Storytime
(206) 684–7539
6801 NE 35th Avenue

Queen Anne Branch–Toddler Storytime
(206) 386–4227
400 W Garfield Street

Southwest Branch–Toddler Storytime
   (206) 684–7455
   9010 SW 35th Avenue

West Seattle Branch–Toddler Storytime
   (206) 684–7444
   2306 SW 42nd Avenue

BOOKSTORES

Many of the chain and independent bookstores have excellent children's departments that are filled with a wide variety of books for youngsters. They also have storytime available to children of all ages. There usually is not an age requirement for storytime; however, you need to be the judge of your own baby's ability to sit and listen. Fortunately, if your child gets restless you can get up and walk around and look at all the books available for purchase.

The following bookstores have storytimes for young children. Those that have a preferred age for their attendees are not listed here.

All for Kids Books and Music
   (206) 526–2768
   2900 NE Blakely Street, Seattle

Barnes and Noble
   (425) 771-2200
   19401 Alderwood Mall Parkway, Lynnwood
   (425) 644-1650
   15600 NE 8th Avenue, Bellevue
   (425) 451–8463
   626 NE 106th Avenue, Bellevue
   (206) 575–3965
   300 W Andover Park, Tukwila 2
   (206) 517–4107
   2675 NE University Village, Seattle
   (425) 398-1990
   18025 Garden Way NE, Woodinville

Borders Books
   (425) 776-7530
   3000 184th Street SW, Lynnwood
   (425) 869-1907
   16549 NE 74th Street, Redmond
Read My Books
   (425) 368-2305
   720 238th Street SE #D, Country Village, Bothell
The Secret Garden
   (206) 789–5006
   6115 NW 15th Avenue, Ballard
Third Place Books
   (206) 366–3333
   17171 NE Bothell Way, Lake Forest Park
   (206) 525-2347
   6504 20th Avenue NE, Seattle
University Bookstore
   (425) 462-4500
   990 102nd Avenue NE, Bellevue
   (425) 385-3530
   15311 Main Street, Mill Creek

PUBLIC SWIMMING POOLS

Swim lessons for babies and toddlers begin at four to six months old, and run up to three or four years old. This is a fine

way to get your child accustomed to the water in a warm pool with other young children and parents. I found that the morning classes are filled with women and babies and the evening classes have mostly men with their children. The locker room floors can be cold, so be prepared. Most pools offer pay lockers and changing tables. Babies need swim

diapers or cloth diapers with rubber diaper pants to prevent unwanted spills. Bring a polyester top to help keep your baby warm. When my child could not walk I brought my stroller, where he waited while we changed our clothes. Classes last half an hour and usually cost about $3-4 per class, with six to eight classes per session. Many of the pools have a family swim open to children of all ages, with no registration necessary.

Ballard Pool
  (206) 684–4094
  1471 NW 67th Street, Ballard
  Evening classes available

Bellevue Aquatics Center
  (425) 452–4444
  601 NE 143rd Avenue, Bellevue
  Evening and weekend classes available

Coleman Pool (outdoors)
  (206) 684–7494
  8603 SW Fauntleroy Way, West Seattle

Evans Pool
  (206) 684–4961
  7201 E Green Lake Drive, Green Lake
  Evening and weekend classes available

Helene Madison Pool
  (206) 684–4979
  13401 N Meridian Avenue, Lake City
  Evening classes available

Issaquah's Julius Boehm Pool
  (425) 837–3350
  50 SE Clark Street, Issaquah

Lynnwood Recreation Center Pool
  (425) 771-4030
  18900 44th Avenue West
  Evening and weekend classes available

Meadowbrook Pool
  (206) 684–4989
  10515 NE 35th Avenue, Lake City

Medgar Evers Pool
  (206) 684–4766
  500 E 23rd Avenue, Central
  Evening and weekend classes available

Mounger Pool (outdoors)
    (206) 684–4708
    2535 W 32nd Avenue, Magnolia
    Evening classes available

Mountlake Terrace Recreation Pavilion Pool
    (425) 776-9173
    5303 228th Street SW, Mountlake Terrace
    Evening classes available

Peter Kirk Pool (outdoors)
    (425) 828–1235
    380 NE Kirkland Avenue, Kirkland

Queen Anne Aquatic Center
    (206) 386–4282
    1920 W 1st Avenue, Queen Anne
    Evening and weekend classes available

Rainier Beach Pool
    (206) 386–1944
    8825 S Rainier Avenue, South Seattle
    Evening and weekend classes available

Redmond City Pool
    (206) 296–2961
    17535 NE 104th Avenue NE, Redmond
    Evening classes available

Shoreline Pool
    (206) 362-1307
    19030 1st Avenue NE, Shoreline
    Evening and weekend classes available

Southwest Pool
    (206) 684–7440
    2801 SW Thistle, South Seattle
    Evening classes available

Yost Park Pool (outdoors)
    (425) 775-2645 or (425) 771-1246
    9535 Bowdoin Way, Edmonds
    Evening and weekend classes available

PRIVATE SWIMMING POOLS

As with public pools, private swimming pools or private lessons offer an excellent way for babies to get used to the water. The pools are kept warm and the class sizes are kept to a minimum. Prices vary and sometimes there is an additional registration or annual membership fee. Call for times and fees.

Ballard Olympic Athletic Club
   (206) 789-5010
   www.olympicathleticclub.com
   5301 Leary Avenue NW, Ballard

Bellevue Family YMCA
   (425) 746–9900
   14230 Bel-Red Road, Bellevue

Kid Swim
   (206) 364–7946
   14540 NE Bothell Way, Lake City

Safe 'N Sound Swimming
   (206) 285–9279 www.snsswim.com
   2040 N Westlake Avenue, Queen Anne

Sammamish Family YMCA
   (425) 391-4840
   4221 228th Avenue SE, Issaquah

Waterbabies Aquatic Program
   (425) 643–4334 www.waterbabies.net
   First Street Fitness, 10001 NE 1st Street, Bellevue
   Classes offered in Bellevue, Issaquah, Kirkland, Sammamish
   and Everett.

West Coast Family Aquatic Center
   (425) 745-3474 www.swimwca.org/facility
   15622 Country Club Drive, Mill Creek

West Seattle Family YMCA
   (206) 935-6000
   4515 36th Avenue SW

Central Seattle

Central Seattle, the heart of the city, includes the neighborhoods of Capitol Hill, Eastlake, Downtown, Madison Park, Magnolia and Queen Anne. Parents will find an exciting range of things to do with their child in this busy section of the city.

BAY PAVILLION CAROUSEL

www.pier57seattle.com

(206) 623–8600
Pier 57, 1301 Alaskan Way, Downtown

Hours: Daily 11 a.m.–8 p.m.

Fees: $1.50 per child

Access: Lot or metered street parking (25¢ per 15 minutes, 2 hours maximum); stroller access

Weekend/evening hours: Yes

Features: Restrooms, food and drink

No changing table, no nursing privacy, no play equipment for tots

A carousel's colorful lights and sounds may stimulate a younger infant, but an actual ride is best for babies who can sit up. Summertime brings hordes of tourists to this area, so if you want a hassle-free visit, go during the winter on a weekday. I found the place empty on winter weekdays and we were allowed to ride as long as we wanted. Activity picks up in the evenings, and it increases even more on weekends. On your way back to your car you will find the Seattle Sourdough Bakery, where you can pick up an excellent roll for the ride home if your little one has started eating solids.

CHILDREN'S MUSEUM

www.thechildrensmuseum.org

(206) 441–1768
305 Harrison Street, Seattle Center House, Lower Level, Seattle

Hours: Monday–Friday 10 a.m.–5 p.m., Saturday and Sunday 10 a.m.–6 p.m.

Fees: Children and adults $7.50, Grandparents and those over 55 $6.50, under one free, annual pass starts at $40.

Access: Lot and street parking; stroller access

Classes: Offered mostly to children over three

Weekend/evening hours: Yes

Features: Play equipment for tots (see below), restrooms, changing table, food and drink (Food Pavilion upstairs); no nursing privacy

The Children's Museum is designed for older infants, toddlers and older children. This museum has a wonderful open layout and boasts seven permanent exhibits. The most appropriate  exhibit for the three and under set is "Discovery Bay." In this fully enclosed area, toddlers can explore an undersea theme that has been specifically designed for their age group. There is an aquarium, tunnels, soft climbing structures, and a stream with plastic water animals that allow some hands on fun. Another exhibit that offers fun learning for your toddler is the "Local Neighborhood." Children can role-play with a child-sized Metro bus, fire engine, grocery store, post office and Mexican Café. The best value is buying a year's membership if you think you will go often.

COOPERATIVE PRESCHOOLS

See Multiple Locations, pages 20–22.

GARFIELD FAMILY CENTER

www.cityofseattle.net/parks

(206) 461–4486

Garfield Community Center
2323 E Cherry Street, Central

Hours: Open Monday–Friday 9 a.m.–5 p.m.; Play & Learn Tuesdays and Thursdays 10:30 a.m.–12:30 p.m.

Access: Parking; stroller access

Classes: Play & Learn (toddler–5 years) free; call or check website for seasonal classes

Features: Play equipment for tots, restrooms, changing table, nursing privacy, food and drink in vending machines, playground outside the center (see page 84)

Play & Learn. Storytime, arts and crafts and school readiness are a part of this program.

LISTENING MOTHERS

www.listeningmothers.org

(206) 275-0104 Seattle or **(425) 450-4332** Bellevue

Hours and fees: Call or go online for class locations; $96 for an 8-week session

Access: Parking; stroller access

Features: Restrooms, changing tables

Listening Mothers is a support group for new mothers with babies 6 weeks and older. Sessions last 90 minutes and are hosted by professionals such as psychologists, social workers, counselors and doulas, all of whom are trained in infant social and emotional development. Participation is kept to a small group, usually about seven mothers and their babies in each group. Listening Mothers focuses on six areas of development: Clarity, Insight, Awareness, Confidence, Knowledge and Understanding.

MAGNOLIA COMMUNITY CENTER

www.cityofseattle.net/parks

(206) 386–4235
2550 W 34th Avenue, Magnolia

Hours: Monday–Friday 10 a.m.–10 p.m. and Saturday 9 a.m.–5 p.m.; call for class times

Access: Parking; stroller access

Classes: Tot Gym (under 5 years) $3 drop-in fee, Tot Bop (1½–3½ years) $35 for two months

Weekend/evening hours: No

Features: Restrooms (small), food and drink in vending machines, playground outside the center (see page 89)

No play equipment for tots, no changing table, no nursing privacy

The Magnolia Community Center is located next to a grade school.

The center offers several options for those under three:

Tot Bop. Songs, music and props are used to get parents and toddlers moving about. It meets once a week for forty-five minutes.

Tot Gym. During this class the gym is closed to everyone except parents and children. Unfortunately, no equipment or toys are provided by the center, so parents must bring their own. This program is ongoing.

MY COFFEE HOUSE

(206) 568-7509

2818 E Madison Street, Madison Park

Hours: Daily 7 a.m.–6 p.m.

Access: Street parking; stroller access

Features: Restrooms with changing tables, no nursing privacy

My Coffee House is a coffee-drinking parent's dream! The set up is perfect when you need some java and a snack, but your little one needs to get out of the house. There is an almost fully enclosed area with benches, couches and a table and chairs for you to relax on while your child plays with the vast array of toys provided. There are bins and bins of all types of toys—blocks, cars, rattles, balls, dinosaurs, and even a train table and kid-sized ballet mirror and bar. Up a few stairs in the same area is a child's reading area with all sorts of books to choose from. My Coffee House serves bagels and pastries in addition to kid friendly snacks such as Cheerios.

PACIFIC SCIENCE CENTER

www.pacsci.org

(206) 443-2001

200 Second Avenue N, Seattle Center, Downtown

Hours: 10 a.m.–5 p.m. daily and Saturday and Sunday 10 a.m.–6 p.m.

Fees: Adults 12–64 $10, children 3-12 $7, seniors 65+ $8.50, under 3 free, annual pass $75

Access: Parking lots (fee) and street (metered); stroller access

Weekend/evening hours: Yes

Features: Just for Tots (see below), restrooms, changing table, nursing privacy, food and drink in Food Pavilion

The Pacific Science Center museum is primarily for older children; however, it has a great play area called Just for Tots, available for toddlers and babies. This space is developed specifically for children who are less than 44 inches tall. A large trough of water is filled with toys used for water play,  a low maze is fun to explore, and plastic slides and climbers are on hand. Adjoining this space are two smaller rooms with more toys and a private nursing area.

The rest of the Pacific Science Center is filled with learning exhibits for adults and older children. The Food Pavilion, located on the Seattle Center grounds, offers a variety of foods.

REI DOWNTOWN STORE

www.rei.com

(206) 223-1944

222 N Yale Avenue, Downtown

Hours: Monday–Friday 10 a.m.–9 p.m., Saturday and Sunday 10 a.m.–7 p.m.

Access: Garage (for a fee) and free street parking; stroller access

Weekend/evening hours: Yes

Features: Play equipment for tots (see below), restrooms, changing table, nursing privacy in women's restroom, food and drink at World Wrapps concession inside, espresso cart outside.

What a fun place to visit with your toddler! This huge store can be very exciting. Before entering the store your little one can gaze at the waterfall outside. Then once inside he or she

can view the giant fiberglass climbing rock, bronze animal tracks and an oversized glass compass embedded in the floor. Upstairs near World Wrapps is a toddler play area. The play equipment features a treehouse, slide and other fun climbing activities. It is worth a visit just to browse, but if you need any type of sporting, camping or biking gear, REI is a great place to shop. Some clothes and shoes are available for older and larger infants. We bought our backpack child carrier and our bike trailer here. Ramps and elevators make stroller use easy, so you can bring your own stroller or use ones that REI provides for older babies. There is even a quiet nursing room in the women's restroom.

SEATTLE AQUARIUM

www.seattleaquarium.org

(206) 386–4320

1483 Alaskan Way, (Pier 59 Waterfront Park), Downtown

Hours: Open Daily. April-May 9:30 a.m.-5 p.m.; May-September 9:30 a.m.–7 p.m.; September-March 10 a.m.–5 p.m.

Fees: Adults $12, children 6–12 $8, children 3–5 $5, 2 years and under free, annual pass starts at $60

Access: Lot or metered street parking (25¢ per 15 minutes, 2 hours maximum); stroller access

Weekend/evening hours: Yes

Features: Restrooms, changing table, nursing privacy, food and drink nearby

No play equipment for tots

The Seattle Aquarium is a good place to take a baby old enough to sit in a stroller. The entire museum is ramped, making

stroller use a breeze, and most of the fish tanks begin at floor level, so you can push the baby right up to the tank for close viewing. My infant enjoyed looking at all the different sizes and colors of fish. Sea mammals are housed in glass tanks that open to the fresh air. Winter seems to hold the crowds down. Groups of children occasionally come for field trips during the school year; however, the aquarium is big enough for you to avoid these groups if you wish. I moved through the entire museum in an hour and a half with baby riding happily along in the stroller. The restroom farther into the aquarium has a handicap stall that will fit a stroller.

SEATTLE PUBLIC LIBRARIES: Toddler Storytime

Queen Anne Branch, Montlake Branch; see Multiple Locations, pages 27–29.

SWIMMING POOLS: Tot Swim

Medgar Evers Pool, Mounger Pool, Queen Anne Aquatic Center, Safe 'N Sound Swimming; see Multiple Locations, pages 30–33.

URBAN MONKEYS

www.gourbanmonkeys.com

(206) 262-9282

1124 Harrison Street, Seattle

Hours and fees: Hours vary depending on the season, $199 annual membership, classes and camps are an additional fee; call or check the website for classes, times and fees. Classes rotate quarterly.

Access: Parking; stroller access

Classes: As many as 16 classes are offered at any given time. Those geared towards young infants include: Nurturing Pathways (6 weeks-24 months), Infant Sign Language, Infant Massage and Baby to Belly and Back. Classes geared toward toddlers include: Little

Monkey Movement (12-24 months) and Run, Wiggle and Giggle (2-3 years).

Features: Women's and men's restrooms with changing tables in each, shower in the women's restroom, snacks and beverages, free wireless internet with membership, lounge with TV and current reading material

Urban Monkeys is a self-described "Jungle for Kids, Oasis for Grownups." Not only do they offer an open play gym and classes for you and/or your child, they also have a spa! Massages, facials, waxing and nail services are available while your older child plays or takes a class. If you join, you'll get the most bang for your membership buck via discounts on classes and through the use of the open gym if your child is mobile. If you choose not to join, you may still sign up for classes.

Nurturing Pathways. In this class, little ones are encouraged to find different ways to move. Balls, instruments and other props are integral parts of baby's self-discovery.

Infant Sign Language. Learn how to communicate with your baby long before your baby is able to verbalize his or her needs and feelings.

Infant Massage. This class teaches how to nurture and promote the good health of your baby through touch.

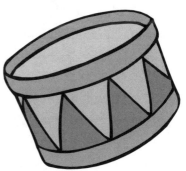

Baby to Belly and Back. This exercise class is aimed at helping new mothers regain tone and strength in their abdomen, back and pelvic floor.

Little Monkey Movement. Stretching, dancing, singing, playing and playing make up this parent/child class that teaches basic dance concepts and develops coordination skills.

Run, Wiggle and Giggle. In this class, toddlers use props and musical instruments to learn to move their body.

If you want to try a class without committing to the whole session, you may pay the drop-in class fee to see if the class meets your and your child's needs. You'll receive a second class free when you do pay the drop-in class fee.

North Seattle

This section of Seattle includes the northeast neighborhoods of Laurelhurst, Green Lake, Wallingford, Lake City and View Ridge, among others, and the northwest neighborhoods of Ballard, Fremont, Phinney Ridge, Loyal Heights and Crown Hill. Shoreline, a city north of Seattle, is also included in this chapter.

ALL FOR KIDS BOOKS AND MUSIC: Storytime

See Multiple Locations, pages 27–29.

ALL THAT DANCE

www.all-that-dance.com

(206)524–8944

8507 NE 35th Avenue, Laurelhurst

Access: Parking; stroller access

Hours and fees: Call for times and fees

Classes: Toddler Creative Movement (2–4 years); 16-week format starting at $210 or $14 to drop in for one hour

Weekend/evening hours: Nothing offered for tots

Features: Restrooms, Take 5 Espresso offers drinks and snacks

No play equipment for tots, no changing table, no nursing privacy

In these classes, a small group of children two to four years old, with their parents, gathers together for movement, dancing and songs. This lightly-structured class offers an opportunity for youngsters to get accustomed to dancing and dance studios.

BALLARD COMMUNITY CENTER

www.ci.seattle.wa.us/parks

(206) 684–4093

6020 NW 28th Avenue, Ballard

Access: Parking; stroller access

Hours and fees: Monday–Friday 10 a.m.–10 p.m. and Saturday 9 a.m.–3 p.m.; Toddler Gym Time $2; call for other class times and fees

Classes: Toddler Play Room (under 4 years); Toddler Gym Time (under 5 years); Fun With Friends (2–3 years); Morning Step It Up Aerobics

Weekend/evening hours: Yes, playroom may open on Saturdays

Features: Play equipment for tots (playground page 101, restrooms, food and drink in vending machines

No changing table, no nursing privacy

Toddler Gym Time. The center has turned its game room into a toddler room replete with riding toys, books, mats and

a slide. Although it is a little small, it does not get too crowded, and provides an enjoyable place to play and meet others.

Tot Drop. The center opens its gym for children of all ages, with their parents, to run and play providing balls and mats. Parents are welcome to bring their own playthings. This arrangement is perfect for groups that don't want to offer their living rooms as meeting places, but still want to get together. When I visited the center, there were about twenty two- to three-year-olds.

Morning Step It Up Aerobics. Childcare is available for mothers taking this one hour low-impact aerobics class.

See the Ballard Community Center playground description, page 101.

BALLARD FAMILY CENTER

(206) 706–9645

5334 Tallman Avenue NW, Ballard

Access: Parking; stroller access

Hours and fees: Monday 1–5 p.m., Tuesday–Thursday 10 a.m.–5 p.m., Friday 10 a.m.–3 p.m.; call for class times and fees

Classes: Playroom (all ages); Kindermusik (0–18 months); Music and Storytime (all ages); Moms on the Move (infants); PEPS Parent/Child Activity Time (0–3 years)

Features: Play equipment for tots (see below), restrooms, changing table, food and drink nearby, nursing privacy

Located in the heart of the Ballard shopping district, this family center has plenty of activities for children under three.

Playroom. The small playroom is open at various times during the week for drop-in playtime. Toys and books are available for your child.

Kindermusik. These classes are a fine way to introduce your baby to music.

Music and Storytime. Singing, finger play and listening to music are the focus of this activity group.

Moms on the Move. This post-partum and pre-natal aerobics class for moms and their babies and is a great way to get back to exercising after having your baby.

Parent/Child Activity Time. This two-hour activity group is open to parents with children under three years old, although exceptions are made for siblings. The group begins with play-time while the facilitator leads an informal discussion with the parents. Snacks, crafts and singing are also part of the program.

BALLARD OLYMPIC ATHLETIC CLUB

(206) 789–5010

5301 Leary NW Avenue, Ballard

Access: Parking; stroller access

Hours and fees: Health club is open 24 hours a day except Saturday and Sunday; call for class times and fees

Classes: Moms and More Aerobics (babies in car seats, or additional fee for childcare). Tot Swim, see page 40.

Weekend/evening hours: Yes

Features: Play equipment for tots in daycare only, restrooms, changing table, food and drink, nursing privacy

Mothers do not have to be members of the athletic club to enroll in their low-impact aerobics class, and they are encouraged to bring their babies if they are not crawling. Mothers with toddlers and crawling babies are encouraged to leave the children with competent caregivers in the nursery on the first floor.

This is a fully equipped health club with a great deal to offer in addition to aerobics. Stop by for a tour of the facilities if membership interests you.

BARNES AND NOBLE: Storytime

See Multiple Locations, pages 29–30.

BITTER LAKE COMMUNITY CENTER

(206) 684–7524

13035 N Linden Avenue, Bitter Lake

Access: Parking; stroller access

Hours and fees: Monday–Thursday 9 a.m.–9 p.m., Friday 9 a.m.–6 p.m., Saturday 9 a.m.–5 p.m.; Toddler Open Gym $1; Brain Play free, donations appreciated; call to confirm current classes and fees

Classes: Toddler Open Gym (under 5 years); Brain Play (birth–3 years)

Weekend/evening hours: Nothing offered for tots

Features: Play equipment for tots (see below), restrooms, changing table, food and drink in vending machines

No nursing privacy

Toddler Open Gym. The center provides balls, scarves, a tunnel, small hoops, and a mat for tumbling. The gym is open to toddlers for two hours, twice a week.

Brain Play. This free and ongoing session encourages activities, play and discussions about ongoing development.

See the Bitter Lake Park description, page 93.

COOPERATIVE PRESCHOOLS

See Multiple Locations, pages 23–24.

CREATIVE DANCE CENTER

www.creativedance.org

(206) 363–7281
   12577 N Densmore Avenue, Haller Lake

Access: Parking; stroller access

Hours and fees: Call for times and fees

Classes: Nurturing Baby (2 months–pre-walking); Parent/Toddler (walking–2 ½ years); Parent/Child/Toddler (18 months–4 years)

Weekend/evening hours: Yes

Features: Restrooms

No play equipment for tots, no changing table, no food or drink available, no nursing privacy

At the Creative Dance Center, parents and children use music, props and instruments in classes to explore movement and dance. The hour-long class is designed to be fun in addition to being educational. The Haller Lake location is in the same building as the Haller Lake Community Club. The Phinney Ridge location is in the Phinney Neighborhood Center at 6532 N Phinney Avenue.

DANCE FREMONT

www.dancefremont.com

(206) 633-0812
   4015 Stone Way N, Fremont

Access: Parking; stroller access

Hours and fees: Call for times, $35 and up

Classes: Nurturing Pathways (2 months-walking); Waddlers (walking-24 months); Toddlers (2-3 years)

Features: Props for tots (see below), restrooms

No changing table, no food or drink available, no nursing privacy

The instructor at Dance Fremont is a developmental specialist and involves parents and children in movement, dance, props and singing.

FAMILY WORKS

www.familyworksseattle.org

(206) 694–6727
1501 N 45th Avenue, Wallingford

Access: Parking; stroller access

Hours and fees: Monday–Friday 9 a.m.–5 p.m.; Everybody's Playgroup (infants and up) Wednesday and Friday 10–11:30 a.m.; Music & Movement (infants–4 years) Tuesday 12:30 p.m.–1 p.m.; Play & Learn (infants–4 years) Thursday 2–3:30 p.m.

Features: Play equipment for tots (see below), restrooms, changing table, food and drink nearby

No nursing privacy

Everybody's Playgroup. Toys, Legos® and books are provided in a clean, carpeted room perfect for rainy days. Play, read and sing with your and other babies. Snacks are provided. Babies can intermingle with toddlers without the threat of being run over by a rolling toy.

Music & Movement. Children and parents explore songs, games, music and dance using a variety of instruments.

Play & Learn. Discover the joy of playing and learning with your child.

GRACEWINDS PERINATAL SERVICES

www.gracewindsperinatal.com

(206) 781-9871
1421 NW 70th Street, Ballard

Access: Street parking, stroller access

Hours and fees: Call for class times. Moms in the Zone (moms plus infants/toddlers) $110 for 8-class punch, $60 for 4-class punch or $15 for drop-in; Infant Massage (parent plus infant) $70 per 4-week session

Features: Restrooms, changing tables, nursing privacy (a clinic with lactation nurses is onsite)

Moms in the Zone. This post-partum class is designed to help new mothers rebuild their pelvic floor and abdominal muscles. Taking place both indoors and out, this class allows you to bring your new baby with you while you focus on getting back into shape. A stroller is a required accessory for this class.

Infant Massage. In this ninety-minute class, you'll learn how to bond with your baby through touch. Infant massage can also help relax your baby and improve sleep cycles.

GREEN LAKE COMMUNITY CENTER

www.cityofseattle.net/parks

(206) 684–4961

7201 E Green Lake Drive, Green Lake

Access: Parking (busy); stroller access

Hours and fees: Monday–Friday 10 a.m.–7 p.m. and Saturday 10 a.m.–2:30 p.m

Classes: Toddler Play Center (6 months-5 years)

Weekend/evening hours: Yes

Features: Play equipment for tots (see playground, pages 91–92), restrooms, changing table, food and drink in vending machines

No nursing privacy

Toddler Play Center. This playroom is open during most of the center's hours of operation. It is an advantage to have a playroom available almost all the time, but this one can feel small if there are too many children present. Toys for climbing, riding, rolling and hugging fill up this second-floor room. Some of the toys are broken and dirty, but new ones are introduced often. I did not like taking a pre-walker here because of the numerous older children running around and grabbing toys. A small riding toy that rolls down a track into the play area can pose a danger to babies. On rainy winter days the room is filled with children under five. Despite its flaws, this play center is useful when you absolutely have to get out of the house.

The center is also available for rental for private parties on Saturdays from 2:30 to 4:30 p.m. for $35 per hour plus a $10 booking fee. This is a great place for birthday parties!

See the Green Lake Park description, pages 91–92.

GUILD 45th STREET THEATER/CRYING ROOM

www.landmarktheatres.com

(206) 633–3353

2115 N 45th Avenue, Wallingford

Access: No parking; stroller access

Fees: Before 6 p.m. Adults $7.50; seniors, children and matinee $4.25

Weekend/evening hours: Yes

Features: No play equipment for tots, restrooms, food and drink, nursing privacy

No changing table

Guild 45th Street Theater has a small crying room in its second theater. This older theater venue usually shows art-house movies and foreign films. The theater is ideal for small, sleeping infants, as the films usually are not loud or violent. Unfortunately, parking is tight.

GYMBOREE

See Multiple Locations, pages 22–23.

HOLISTIC YOGA CENTER

www.seattleholisticcenter.com

(206) 547–9882

4649 Sunnyside Avenue N, Room 300, North Seattle

Hours and fees: Call for class times and fees

Access: Parking; stroller access

Classes: Post-Natal Yoga (infants); Infant Massage (pre-crawlers)

Features: Restrooms, nursing privacy, food and drink in vending machines

No changing table

Post-Natal Yoga. Whether you have experienced yoga before or if you are a beginner, this form of exercise is a gentle way to get back into shape. The class requires no registration or commitment. Mothers and infants come only when they feel up to it. The teacher is aware that some mothers have had cesarean sections and require a slower pace. Anywhere from 5 to 23 moms show up at the classes. Mothers are required to be at least four weeks post-partum and can bring babies up to a year old as long as the child is quiet enough to allow the mom to participate in the class.

Infant Massage. This class is ideal for babies with colic. The one-hour class is part of a four-class series. Usually five people attend but there is a limit of ten. Lotion and a book are provided.

LOYAL HEIGHTS COMMUNITY CENTER

www.cityofseattle.net/parks

(206) 684–4052

2101 NW 77th Street, Loyal Heights

Access: Parking; no stroller access

Hours and fees: Monday–Friday 10 a.m.–10 p.m. and Saturday 9 a.m.–2:45 p.m.; call for class times and fees

Classes: Play Center Co-op; Parent/Child Playgroup–Infant/Toddler (infants–24 months); Parent/Child Playgroup–Young Preschooler (2–3 ½ years); Two Day Twos;

Weekend/evening hours: Yes

Features: Play equipment for tots (see playground, page 105), restrooms, changing table

No food or drink available, no nursing privacy

Play Center Co-op Classes. These classes include a structured time for playing, circle time and other activities. Parents are required to stay one day a week, but no other duties are required. Classes for older children have more structure than those for younger toddlers. The Friday Night Co-op enables parents to have one evening out every other Friday. Parents are required to stay a couple evenings in the semester.

Parent/Child Playgroup Classes. This is an excellent place for your child to explore different toys and equipment as well as socialize in a safe environment. For two hours parents and children gather for this informal class. During the first half of the class the children are free to wander about the room playing with toys designed for different ages. Then parents and children gather together for singing. The equipment and toys are clean and safe; everyone is friendly and relaxed.

Two Day Twos. This is a 2 ½ hour cooperative playtime for a maximum of six toddlers. The children are provided toys, activities, crafts and music. Parents are required to share duties and care.

Drop-In Afternoons. The playroom is open for unsupervised play. Parents are required to stay.

See the Loyal Heights Playground description, page 105.

MEADOWBROOK COMMUNITY CENTER

www.cityofseattle.net/parks

(206) 684–7522
10515 NE 35th Avenue, Lake City

Access: Parking; stroller access

Hours and fees: Monday–Friday 9 a.m.–9:30 p.m. and Saturday 9 a.m.–5 p.m.; Playroom open Monday and Friday 10 a.m.–1 p.m. and Wednesday and Thursday 5 p.m.–8 p.m.; Little Tykes Play Gym open Tuesday and Wednesday 10 a.m.–12:30 p.m. Both are $2 per day for drop-in play or $15 per quarter.

Classes: Playroom (6 months-4 years), Little Tykes Play Gym (2–5 years)

Weekend/evening hours: Yes, evenings

Features: Play equipment for tots (see below) restrooms, food and drink in vending machines

No changing table, no nursing privacy

The new community center at Meadowbrook is attached to the old swimming pool building. The facility provides mats, balls, a play kitchen, puzzles and building blocks. Parents are also encouraged to bring their child's own ride-on toys. This arrangement is best for walkers and crawlers, and most of the children are under three. Expect to share your toys because toddlers don't know the meaning of "yours" and "mine."

METRO CINEMAS/CRYING ROOM

(206) 633-0055

4500 NE 9th Avenue, University District

Access: Parking lot with 1-hour validation; stroller access, elevator

Fees: Adults $9.25, children and matinee $6.50

Weekend/evening hours: Yes

Features: Restrooms, food and drink, nursing privacy

No play equipment for tots or changing table

The exterior of this multiplex would lead you to believe it is one large theater. However, the building houses about ten small screens. The crying room, which is adequate, is in the rear of the theater. This movie theater screens many light comedies or family-oriented shows. Give yourself plenty of time to find parking as the lots nearby are often full.

NORTHGATE COMMUNITY CENTER

www.seattle.gov/parks

(206) 386-4283

10510 5th Avenue NE, Northgate

Access: Parking; stroller access

Hours and fees: Monday – Thursday Noon – 9 p.m.; Friday 11 a.m. – 9 p.m.; call for class times and fees

Classes: None for ages under 3 at the time I visited the center

Weekend/evening hours: No

Features: Play equipment for tots (climbers, swings, slides), restrooms, changing tables, a small convenience store located in the center sells food and drink

No nursing privacy, no shade

The Northgate Community Center opened its doors in mid-summer 2006. At the time I visited, the class curriculum was still being developed. I was told that due to popular demand, plans are in place to offer classes for toddlers by winter 2006. Even if classes for toddlers are still being developed at the time you visit, the center is worth a trip to take advantage of the brand new outdoor play area located just north of the building. Another bonus is the center's close proximity to the Northgate Branch of the Seattle Library.

NORTH SEATTLE FAMILY SUPPORT CENTER

(206) 364–7930

3200 NE 125th Street, Suite 2, Lake City

Access: Parking limited; no stroller access

Fees: Monday–Friday 9 a.m.–5 p.m.; call for class times

Classes: PEPS (under 3 years)

Features: Play equipment for tots (see below), restrooms, changing table, snacks provided, nursing privacy

Parent/Child Activity Time. This two-hour activity group is open to parents with children un-

der three, although exceptions are made for siblings. The group starts with open playtime in a large, carpeted room with toys, games and books available for younger children. A facilitator leads an informal discussion with parents, after which crafts are made with the parents' help. A snack served to the youngsters is followed by singing. The class is informal, so don't worry if you are late.

Parent/Child Activity Time is excellent for families with more than one child. It is also good for those moms who are continuing their regular PEPS meetings with their older babies, but do not want to volunteer their house to a group of active toddlers.

RAVENNA-ECKSTEIN COMMUNITY CENTER

www.cityofseattle.net/parks

(206) 684–7534

6535 NE Ravenna Avenue, Ravenna

Access: Parking; stroller access

Hours and fees: Monday and Wednesday 10 a.m.-9 p.m.; Tuesday, Thursday, Friday 1 p.m.-9 p.m.; Saturday 10 a.m.–5 p.m.; call for class times and fees

Classes: Indoor Toddler Playspace (under 5 years); Tot Gym Club (2–5 years); Tiny Tots (2–3 years and 2 ½ –3 ½ years)

Weekend/evening hours: Yes

Features: Play equipment for tots (see below), restrooms, changing table, food and drink in vending machines

No nursing privacy

Indoor Toddler Playspace. A good-sized room contains pieces of large equipment and many toys. I went at 3 p.m. and found about five toddlers; by 4:30 there must have been over twenty. The toys and equipment were in good condition and clean, the room is carpeted and there are mats, especially around the plastic slide. The hours that this room is open varies; call for times.

Tiny Tots. For two hours, twice a

week, you can leave your two-to-three-year-old with an instructor and other children of a similar age. The maximum group size is 12. Games, storytelling, arts and crafts are provided for entertainment. Parents are expected to assist with class duties several times during the session.

Tot Gym Club. Balls, play toys and riding toys are provided. It's okay to bring your child's own car or tricycle to ride on.

SEATTLE GYMNASTICS ACADEMY

www.seattlegymnastics.com

(206) 362-7447
12535 NE 26th Avenue, Lake City

Access: Parking; stroller access

Hours and fees: Call for Parent/Tot class times and fees; Indoor Playground offered Monday–Friday 11:30 a.m.–12:45 p.m.; $4 if your child is enrolled in a class at the academy, $6 if not

Classes: Parent/Tot Class (18 months–3 years), Indoor Playground (1–5 years)

Weekend/evening hours: Yes

Features: Play equipment for tots (see below), restrooms, food and drink in vending machines

No changing table, no nursing privacy

The Seattle Gymnastics Academy is designed for all levels of gymnastics and for participants of all ages. The main room is filled with uneven bars, balance beams, trampolines and apparatuses used to train competitive gymnasts. A smaller room used for the Parent/Tot class has soft tumbling objects perfect for toddlers. Also, there is a small nook near the bleachers you can use for babies who have siblings in other classes.

Parent/Tot Class. Although this class is open to children 18 to 36 months, most children participating are 24 months and up. These youngsters do well sitting in a circle and following simple movements. Younger children, unless mature for their age, may have a more difficult time with the structured class. The class begins with singing and bubble blowing. The children then sit in a circle for a short movement game. Then the toddlers are given time to explore the equipment. They are also brought into the large gym where they can play on the trampoline and other apparatuses. Toward the end of the class they jump into a pit filled with foam rubber blocks—it's hard to describe the activity, but the children enjoyed it.

The academy is ideal for parents with slightly older children as well as toddlers, as a class for four and five year olds is offered concurrently. If you wish to encourage your child to be involved in gymnastics, this is an ideal place to start.

Indoor Playground. Supervised by gymnastics instructors, the Indoor Playground offers playtime with hopping, jumping, and balancing on gym equipment for approximately an hour.

SEATTLE PUBLIC LIBRARIES: Toddler Storytime

Green Lake Branch, Northeast Branch, Lake City Branch, Ballard Branch; see Multiple Locations, pages 27–29.

THE SECRET GARDEN

www.secretgardenbooks.com

(206) 789-5060
2214 NW Market Street, Ballard

Access: Parking; stroller access

Hours and fees: Monday–Saturday 10 a.m.–6 p.m., Thursday 10 a.m.–8 p.m., Sunday 1–5 p.m.

Classes: Storytime (any age)

Weekend/evening hours: Yes

Features: Play equipment for tots (see below), restrooms

No changing table, no food or drink, no privacy for nursing

This bookstore provides a delightful alternative to large chain bookstores or public libraries. Convenient angled parking in front of the store allows you to whisk your baby from the car to the store in no time at all. Once inside, you can seat your toddler at the low puzzle table to read books or play with puzzles and games while you rock your infant in a nearby comfortable rocker. There are enough nooks to provide for private nursing, and the bathroom is large enough to lay your changing pad on the floor to change a diaper. The store's knowledgeable staff can help find books suitable for your baby.

SPARTAN RECREATION CENTER

www.cityofshoreline.com/parks

(206) 546–5041
185th Street and 1st Avenue NE, Shoreline

Access: Parking; stroller access

Hours and fees: Call for times and fees

Classes: Indoor Playground (1-5 years), not offered in the summer

Features: Play equipment for tots (see below), restrooms

No changing table, no food or drink available, no nursing privacy

This large gym, which can accommodate up to 100 children at a time, contains toys and equipment for youngsters of varying ages. The center offers slides, teeter-totters, climbing toys, mini basketball hoops and balls. Unfortunately, the center does not open its gym for Indoor Playground during the summer months, so call ahead for times and dates. The Shoreline Center is a large complex of buildings just off 1st Avenue NE. The gym is behind the Center's auditorium on the eastern side of the complex.

SHORELINE FAMILY SUPPORT CENTER

www.chs-nw.org

(206) 362–7282
17018 NE 15th Avenue, Shoreline

Access: Parking; no stroller access

Hours and fees: Monday–Friday 9 a.m.–5 p.m.; call for class times and fees

Classes: Indoor Playground (under 5 years)

Features: Play equipment for tots (see below), restrooms, changing table

No nursing privacy, no food or drink available

The support center opens its preschool room to children under five years old for two hours on Friday. The room is small but it has numerous small toys and games. A low table with chairs is available for reading or crafts.

SWEDISH MEDICAL CENTER

www.swedish.org

(206) 386–3606
1120 Cherry Street, First Hill

(206) 781-6344
5300 NW Tallman Avenue, Ballard

Hours and fees: Call for class times and fees

Access: Parking garage and meters; stroller access

Classes: Moms and Babies Exercise (pre-crawlers)

Features: Restrooms, nursing privacy, food and drink in vending machines

No changing table

Moms and Babies Exercise. This very low impact aerobics class is designed especially for post-partum mothers and their infants. Also included in this one-hour class are stretching and abdominal reconditioning. Because the music is mellow and soft, the babies are not disturbed. Approximately eight to ten moms attend this class along with their pre-crawling infants.

SWIMMING POOLS: Tot Swim

Ballard Pool, Evans Pool, Helene Madison Pool, Meadowbrook Pool, Kid's Swim, Ballard Olympic Athletic Club; see Multiple Locations, pages 30–33.

TOP TEN TOYS

www.toptentoys.com

(206) 782-0098

104 N 85th Street, Crown Hill

Access: Parking; stroller access

Hours: Open Wednesday–Friday 9 a.m.–9 p.m. and Saturday–Tuesday 9 a.m.–7p.m. (hours vary by the season)

Weekend/evening hours: Yes

Features: Play equipment for tots (toys for play and sale), restrooms, food and drink at nearby McDonalds, changing table, nursing privacy

This is not just an ordinary toy store. In addition to having every toy imaginable for all ages of children, there is also an area near the toddler section that has toys for your child to try out. You can see if your baby responds to the toy before purchasing it. The family restroom has a comfortable changing table and child-size toilet for potty-trained children.

TUNE TALES

www.tunetalesmusic.com

(425) 415-1690

1211 NE 168th Place, Bothell

Access: Parking on street; stroller access

Hours and fees: Call for times and fees

Classes: Arpeggios (newborn–1 year), Allegros (1-3 years), Crescendos (3–5 years)

Features: Play equipment for tots (see below), restrooms

No changing table, no nursing privacy

Sign your toddler up for an enjoyable half hour of musical fun. Two animated leaders engage the children by combining old favorite songs and new ones with musical instruments, teddy bears, scarves and more. The children are encouraged to participate with the props and are not pressured stay on their parent's lap. This is a great way to introduce your toddler to music.

UNIVERSITY BOOKSTORE: Storytime

See Multiple Locations, pages 27–28.

Mercer Island, South Seattle, West Seattle

These areas of Seattle can sometimes be a challenge to get to from the main part of the city. Despite this, there are still many terrific things to do and places to go that are geared toward residents of these neighborhoods.

ARENA SPORTS

www.arenasports.net

(206) 782-8606
    4636 E Marginal Way S, #A-100, Georgetown

Hours and fees: Call for class times and fees; fees start at $12.50 per class

Access: Park in the rear; stroller access

Weekend/evening hours: Yes

Classes: Lil' Kickers Soccer (18 months and up)

Features: Restrooms, changing table, food and drink available, privacy for nursing

Arena Sports offers soccer skills programs for children of all ages. There are two programs for toddlers: Bunnies (18 months-24 months) is the introductory level for the Lil' Kickers program. In a 40-minute class, toddlers and parents explore the basics of soccer. Activities also include parachute play, bubbles and lots of goal scoring. The next level is Thumpers (2-3 years). Also 40 minutes long, this program includes organized games to develop listening skills, balance, ball skills and foot-eye coordination.

Arena Sports also is located in Redmond at 9040 Willows Road,(425) 885-4881, and in Magnuson Park at 7727 63rd Avenue NE Suite 101, (206)985-8990. Bonuses of these two locations are the Arena Sports Fun Zones. These inflatable playgrounds are open to all ages and provide a drop-in play area. Call for times; fees are $5 for Arena Sports members and $7 for non-members.

COOPERATIVE PRESCHOOLS

See Multiple Locations, pages 23–24.

DELRIDGE COMMUNITY CENTER

www.ci.seattle.wa.us/parks

(206) 684-7423
4501 SW Delridge Way, West Seattle

Hours and fees: Monday–Friday 10 a.m.–10 p.m. and Saturday 1–8 p.m.; call for class times. $2 except for Wednesdays, which only cost $1

Classes: Toddler Mini Gym (under 5 years)

Access: Parking; stroller access

Features: Play equipment for tots (see playground, page 103–104), restrooms, changing table, food and drink in vending machines

No nursing privacy

A multitude of balls, floor mats, wagons, slide and toys for riding, pushing and climbing await your toddler at this play center. A seated activity center and play-gym are available for young infants as well. Although this gym can accommodate many children, there are ample toys to go around.

MERCER ISLAND BOYS and GIRLS CLUB

www.cmiregistration.com

(206) 232-4548
2825 W Mercer Way, Mercer Island

Hours and fees: Call to confirm class times; $3 per child

Classes: Rainy Day Playground (under 5 years); open Wednesday and Thursday 9:30 a.m.–12 p.m., October-May

Access: Parking; no stroller access

Features: Play equipment for tots (see below), restrooms, changing table, drink in vending machines

No nursing privacy, no food

This large gym is filled with trikes, balls, small slides and tumbling cushions, all perfect for the loads of toddlers that come to play. On cool days the gym can be chilly so bring a sweater. The gym floor is wood so your child can speed around on the tricycles and there is enough room so they do not run into the other children. This gym is open only nine months of the year and may change to only being open on rainy days, so call ahead before you visit.

RAINIER COMMUNITY CENTER

www.ci.seattle.wa.us/parks

(206) 723–8590
4600 S 38th Avenue, Gym #2, South Seattle

Hours and fees: Monday–Thursday 10 a.m.–8 p.m., Friday and Saturday 10 a.m.–5 p.m.; call for class times and fees. Indoor Playground $2

Classes: Indoor Playground

Access: Parking; stroller access

Features: Play equipment for tots (see below), restrooms, changing table, food and drink in vending machines

No nursing privacy

A playroom with toys, blocks and craft supplies is offered. Call for times.

SOUTHWEST FAMILY CENTER

www.swyfs.org

(206) 937–7680
4555 SW Delridge Way, West Seattle

Hours and fees: Monday–Friday 9 a.m.–7 p.m.; call for class times and to confirm playroom availability. Playroom is free

Classes: PEPS Parent/Child Activity Time (under 3 years); Playroom (under 5)

Access: Parking; stroller access

Features: Play equipment for tots (see below), restrooms, changing table, nursing privacy

No food or drink available

The Southwest Family Center has the best playroom in King County. Not only is it filled with toys for all ages, it is also equipped with a kitchen, diaper changing area, television and VCR. Natural light brightens this large, clean room. Couches and chairs provide spots for parents to relax and read the numerous parenting books that are provided while their children are within easy reach. In the mornings, the room is not busy; in the afternoons it serves as a childcare facility for the center's various class participants.

Parent/Child Activity Time. This two-hour activity group is open to parents with children under three years old although exceptions are made for siblings. The group begins with playtime while the facilitator leads an informal discussion with the parents. Snacks, crafts and singing are also a part of the program.

SPECTRUM DANCE THEATER

www.spectrumdance.org

(206) 325–4161

800 Lake Washington Boulevard, Madrona

Classes: Movement with Your Toddler (1–2 years), Movement with Your Toddler 2 (2–3 years), Creative Movement (3–4 years). Movement with Your Toddler requires parent/caregiver attendance; Creative Movement is a child only class

Access: Parking; stroller access

Features: Restrooms

No play equipment for tots, no changing table, no food or drink available, no nursing privacy

Located on Lake Washington, this dance school is co-sponsored by the Seattle Department of Parks and Recreation. The toddler dance classes invite children and their parents to join in play exercises. On nice days you can enjoy the sandy beach located below the building.

SWIMMING POOLS: Tot Swim

Medgar Evers Pool, Mounger Pool, Queen Anne Aquatic Center, Safe 'N Sound Swimming; see Multiple Locations, pages 29–31.

The Eastside

Among the suburbs on the east side of Lake Washington are the popular cities of Bellevue, Medina, Kirkland, Redmond, Issaquah, Woodinville, and Renton. Because these rapidly growing areas boast many families with children, you will find a wealth of indoor activities for your newborn, crawler or toddler.

ANDERSON PARK/REDMOND PARKS AND RECREATION

(425) 556–2300
    7802 NE 168th Avenue, Redmond

Hours and fees: Monday–Friday 8 a.m.–5 p.m.; call for class times and fees

Classes: Kindermusik (Age Groups range from newborn to 3 years); Tiny Treks (2–4 years); Gymnastics – Mighty Mites (18–36 months); Baby Boogie Woogie (1–3 years); Discovery Dance (2–4 years); Two's Toes DancePlay (2–3 years); Indoor Play (0–5 years); Expressive Creations! (1–5 years)

Access: Parking; stroller access

Features: Play equipment for tots (see below), restrooms, food and drink nearby

No changing table, no nursing privacy.

This wooded city park hosts a number of activities in various locations in and around the park. A majority of classes take place at the Old Redmond Schoolhouse. A small playground adorns the southeast tip of the park.

Kindermusik. Introduce your youngster to music and dance  through instruments, puppets and creative movement in a series of classes that focus on the developmental milestones of each age group.

Tiny Treks. These adventures focus on family fun through the exploration of the outdoors and our natural surroundings. Activities may include a short hike, singing, crafts or an outdoor project. These classes may meet at different parks throughout the session.

Gymnastics – Mighty Mites. Parents and their child work together to help the child learn motor, social and emotional development. Gym equipment, foam mats and trampolines play a key role in this class.

Baby Boogie Woogie. Games and songs, dancing and singing are a fun group activity for parent and baby.

Discovery Dance. Dancing and singing and creative movement help young ones build confidence, balance and coordination.

Two's Toes DancePlay. The focus of this class is on movement and fun. This class is self-described as a basis for play at home. Children learn about concepts such as "over, under and through." Take home activities and new ideas each week are included.

Indoor Play. For a $2 drop-in fee, bring your tot to play on ride-on toys, climbing toys, gym mats and other toys. Children under one are free.

Expressive Creations! This is another drop-in class with a different activity each week. Expect music and movement, storytelling, arts and crafts or even drama.

Redmond Park District also sponsors other seasonal and outdoor classes that meet periodically throughout the year. Call (425) 556–2300 for a recreation guide.

See the Anderson Park description, page 132.

BARNES AND NOBLE: Storytime

See Multiple Locations, pages 27–28.

BELLEVUE FAMILY YMCA

(425) 746–9900
14230 Bel-Red Road, Bellevue

Hours and fees: Monday–Thursday 5 a.m.–10 p.m., Friday 5 a.m.–9 p.m., Saturday and Sunday 8 a.m.–6 p.m., call for class times and fees

Classes: Parent/Tot Swim (6 months–3 years)

Weekend/evening hours: Yes

Access: Parking; stroller access

Features: Play equipment for tots (see below), restrooms, changing table, food and drink in vending machines

No nursing privacy

At the Bellevue YMCA, parents accompany their children in the pool for a thirty-minute session. Memberships include a one-time joining fee in addition to a monthly charge. Non-members can participate in the swim lessons for a small fee. The facility offers other programs for adults and older children, but nothing else for toddlers. For $1 an hour, with a two hour maximum, an onsite nursery provides care for your toddler or infant if you are in an aerobic class.

BORDERS BOOKS: Storytime

See Multiple Locations, pages 27–28.

COOPERATIVE PRESCHOOLS

See Multiple Locations, pages 23–24.

CROSSROADS COMMUNITY CENTER

www.ci.bellevue.wa.us

(425) 452–4874
1600 NE 10th Street, Bellevue

Hours and fees: Monday–Friday 9 a.m.–8 p.m. and Saturday 9 a.m.–5 p.m.; call for class times and fees

Classes: Playgroup (under 5 years)

Access: Parking; stroller access

Features: Play equipment for tots (see below), restrooms, food and drink in vending machines

No changing table, no nursing privacy

For two hours on Fridays the Crossroads Community Center opens its large gym to parents with children under five. Usually there are fewer than ten children at any one time. The center provides bikes, balls, toys and mats. Parents are required to set up and take down the equipment.

See the Crossroads Playground description, page 125.

CHILD'S PLAY CAFÉ

www.childsplaycafe.com

(425) 453-6151

10235 Main Street, Bellevue

Hours and fees: Monday–Friday 9 a.m.–3 p.m., Saturday and Sunday reserved for private parties. Walkers: $6.75 for one hour of play, $3.75 per additional half hour; Infants under 6 months: free; Non-walkers: $3.75 per hour and $1.75 per additional half hour. Reservations are recommended.

Access: Parking; stroller access

Features: Play equipment for walkers and non-walkers (see below), restrooms, changing tables (with supplies provided if you need them), nursing privacy, food and drink

The Child's Play Café offers a great place to go and relax, knowing that you don't need to watch your child every second, and that they are in a safe and clean environment.

The café offers several play areas geared toward different age levels and abilities. The biggest play area is supervised, and is aimed primarily at children 18 months or older. There is a slide, mini-ball pit, tool bench, kitchen, ride-on toys, a train and little people table, along with other age appropriate toys. There is also a pretend play area, a quiet area for younger children, and an ocean room with a giant climb-on boat, aquarium and other interactive activities.

You are requested not to bring your own food into the Child's Play Café, which is perfectly fine, since they offer a wonderful menu of healthy food for adults and kids. Bagels, fresh fruit, vegetables, Goldfish crackers are just some of the offerings, and Cheerios are always complimentary.

EVERGREEN COMMUNITY HEALTH CARE

www.evergreenhealthcare.org

(425) 899–3000

12040 NE 128th Street, Kirkland

Hours and fees: Call for class times and fees

Access: Parking; stroller access

Classes: The Happiest Baby on the Block (0-4 months), Nurturing Moms Support Group (newborn and up)

Features: Restrooms, nursing privacy, changing table, food and drink in cafeteria

The Happiest Baby on the Block. This class is based on the book by Dr. Harvey Karp and teaches the approaches he advocates to keep your baby happy. His focus is primarily on how soothe a fussy baby in minutes or less.

Nurturing Moms Support Group. This group meets once per month and focuses on helping moms that are struggling with breastfeeding.

Evergreen Hospital also offers other special interest classes on occasion, such as Infant Massage or Postpartum Yoga. Call the Evergreen Health Line to inquire about other seminars on various topics of interest.

GYMBOREE

See Multiple Locations, pages 24–25.

HIGHLAND COMMUNITY CENTER

(425) 452–7686 www.ci.bellevue.wa.us

14224 Bel-Red Road, Bellevue

Hours and fees: Monday–Thursday 9 a.m.–8 p.m., Friday and Saturday 9 a.m.–5 p.m.

Classes: Open gym (under 5 years) offered the third week of September through second week of June from 9–11:30 a.m. weekdays except Tuesday; $2.50 per child for Bellevue residents, $3 per child for non-residents

Weekend/evening hours: Nothing offered for tots

Access: Parking; stroller access

Features: Play equipment for tots (see below), restrooms, food and drink in vending machines

No changing table, no nursing privacy

This community center offers a large gym filled with all sorts of toys for children under five. It's perfect for rainy days—take your toddler here for running, riding and playing with a wide variety of items. The center does not offer any specialized classes for toddlers and infants but this open gym makes up for the loss.

ISSAQUAH COMMUNITY CENTER

www.ci.issaquah.wa.us

(425) 837–3300

301 S Rainier Boulevard, Issaquah

Hours and fees: Monday-Friday 6 a.m.–10 p.m., Saturday 8 a.m.– 1 p.m., hours may change seasonally; call for quarterly class offerings

Classes: Indoor Playground (1–3 years) 8–11:45 a.m. Monday–Friday, $2 per child

Weekend/evening hours: Nothing offered for tots

Access: Parking; stroller access

Features: Play equipment for tots (see below), restrooms, changing table, food and drink in vending machines

No nursing privacy

From the outside, the Issaquah Community Center looks more like an expensive health club than a city community center; inside, the facilities are just as nice. Most of the activities are housed in the huge carpeted gym that is divided into three sections.

Indoor Playground. Toddlers enjoy one-third of the large gym to play with the bikes, slides and many other toys that the center provides. Carpeting makes any falls a little softer.

ISSAQUAH DEPOT MUSEUM

www.issaquahhistory.org

(425) 392–2322
50 Rainier Boulevard N, Issaquah

Hours and fees: Friday–Sunday 11 a.m.–3 p.m. (June 1–August 31), $2 adults, $1 children; Thursday 4–8 p.m., free

Weekend/evening hours: Yes

Access: Parking; stroller access

Features: Restrooms

No play equipment for tots: no changing table, no food or drink available, no nursing privacy

Two sets of railroad tracks straddle this small museum. Located in a replica of a train station, it houses logging train memorabilia, historical facts and artifacts of a time gone by. An old caboose, passenger train and a couple of other industrial trains that sit in front of the museum are available to explore. When the museum is closed, the trains can still be viewed.

MOTHERS AND OTHERS

www.stmadsophie.com

(425) 226-6600
St. Madeline Sophie Catholic Church
4400 SE 130th Place, Rooms J, K and L, Bellevue

Hours and fees: Call for time and fees for meetings

Classes: Support group, childcare available

Access: Parking; stroller access

Features: Play equipment for tots (see below), restrooms, changing table, nursing privacy

No food or drink available

Mothers, fathers and caregivers are welcome to meet two hours weekly for informative discussions, speakers and activities. During the school year, between 25 and 60 mothers, fathers, grandparents and nannies gather once a week at the church. Children are left with caregivers while the parents meet separately. Infants are cared for in one area, toddlers play together in a separate room and preschoolers experience a more structured class. You may keep your baby with you if necessary. In the summer, the group meets at various parks in the area. The facilitators also organize Mom's Night Out and family events.

MY GYM

www.my-gym.com

(425) 451-1393
900 160th Avenue NE, Suite 1-2, Bellevue

Hours and fees: Call for class times and fees. Ten-week sessions start at $155.

Classes: Tiny Tikes (3-11 months), Waddlers (12-18 months), Gymsters (19 months-2½ years), Terrific Tots (2½ -3½ years)

Access: Parking; stroller access

Features: Restrooms (including stools for children to access sinks), changing table, nursing privacy

My Gym's classes focus on building strength, coordination and social skills. Their programs are non-competitive and consist of games, relays, gymnastics, music and dance.

Most sessions have a five to one student/teacher ratio, which makes their program especially appealing. The equipment is rearranged weekly to keep things interesting and challenging.

NORTH KIRKLAND COMMUNITY CENTER

www.ci.kirkland.wa.us

(425) 587-3350
12421 NE 103rd Avenue, Kirkland

Hours and fees: Monday–Friday 8 a.m.–5 p.m. Open for classes on Saturday; call for seasonal classes, times and fees

Classes: Indoor Playground (1–5 years) $2 per child; Nurturing Pathways® for Babies (2 months–pre-walking); Baby Boogie Woogie (12–36 months); Pee Wee Singing (2-4 years); Parent/Child How Does Your Garden Grow? (2-3 years); Parent/Child Motion (12–20 months, 18–26 months, and 18–34 months); Parent/Child Art (2–3 years); Parent/Child Someone's in the Kitchen (2–3 years)

Weekend/evening hours: Yes

Access: Parking; stroller access

Features: Play equipment for tots (see below), restrooms, changing table, food and drink in vending machines

No nursing privacy

This small community center has a large number of activities for youngsters.

Indoor Playground. Toys and games are available for youngsters. The playground is closed during Lake Washington School District's breaks, so call ahead to see if the playground is open and at what times.

Nurturing Pathways® for Babies. Enrich your baby's development, learn fun activities for tummy time and stimulate your baby's motor skills in this one-hour parent/child class.

Baby Boogie Woogie. This musical class introduces your toddler and you to all of the old song favorites in addition to making music with fun instruments.

Pee Wee Singing. Hop, sing, clap and dance to welcome and goodbye songs. The instructor of this class brings her guitar and guides children in the development of musical skills.

Parent/Child How Does Your Garden Grow? This is a hands-on exploration of gardening, nature, bugs and more. Projects include planting, crafts and outdoor observation.

Parent/Child Motion. A series of classes in which your child will meet friends, build confidence and have fun. Crawling, climbing, balancing, bouncing and other age-appropriate activities will encourage the development of your child's motor skills.

Parent/Child Art. Make art with your child using paint, paper, clay and other fun materials.

Parent/Child Someone's in the Kitchen. Each class has a recipe of the day that allows children to participate. What fun for children who love to help Mommy or Daddy make dinner!

See the North Kirkland Park description, page 138

NORTHWEST ARTS CENTER

www.ci.bellevue.wa.us

(425) 452–6046
9825 NE 24th Street, Bellevue

Hours and fees: Monday–Friday 8 a.m.–5 p.m.; call to confirm class times and fees

Classes: Pee Wee Picasso (18 months–2½ years); Romp and Roll (18 months–2½ years); Messy Hands (2–3 years); Baby Beethoven (18 months-2½ years); numerous other classes offered seasonally—call or go online for availability

Access: Parking; stroller access

Features: Play equipment for tots (see below), restrooms, changing table

No nursing privacy, no food or drink available

This center primarily consists of classrooms; however, its diminutive size in no way minimizes the opportunities for children under three.

Pee Wee Picasso. Up to eight toddlers experiment with different crafts. Four low tables are set with different activities for the little ones. An instructor who is assisted by parents leads the forty-five minute class.

Romp and Roll. For forty-five minutes your tot uses exercise and singing to emphasize coordination, listening and social skills. The class is kept small, with a maximum of ten children, each with a parent.

Messy Hands. This is a hands-on art class for you and your child. You'll both get your hands dirty with different art mediums and make some original creations.

Baby Beethoven. In this class, you and your child will try different rhythm instruments, sing songs and incorporate movement in an introduction to classical music.

OVERLAKE HOSPITAL MEDICAL CENTER

www.overlakehospital.org

(425) 688–5259

1035 116th Avenue NE, Bellevue

Hours and fees: Call or go online for class times, locations and fees

Access: Parking; stroller access

Classes: You and Your New Baby (begins when infants are 4-6 weeks old); Conscious Fathering: After the Baby Arrives (4-6 weeks to 12 weeks); Infant Massage (3 months-crawling)

Features: Restrooms, changing table, nursing privacy

No food or drink

You and Your New Baby. Between 12 and 15 mothers with their infants meet for two hours once a week for five weeks in this class. The time is spent helping with the transition to parenthood. Topics include comforting baby, infant nutrition, dealing with changing family roles and how to help stimulate your infant's development. This class is geared to new mothers; however, dads are welcome also.

Conscious Fathering: After the Baby Arrives. Dads take their young infants to this ninety-minute class to learn about the transition from couplehood to parenthood and learn supportive skills for the mother.

Infant Massage: This class teaches you how to nurture your baby through touch. Claimed benefits of infant massage include helping your baby's digestion, relaxation and sleep.

RENTON COMMUNITY CENTER

www.ci.renton.wa.us

(425) 235-2560

1715 Maple Valley Highway, Renton

Hours and fees: Hours: Monday–Thursday 9 a.m.–9 p.m., Friday and Saturday 10 a.m.–6 p.m.; call for class times and fees

Classes: Kindermusik Village (newborn–18 months); Terrific Tots Playground (10 months–3 years); Messy Time for 2's (2 years); Parent/Infant Class (newborn–6 months); Toddlersize (2–3 years)

Weekend/evening hours: Yes

Access: Parking; stroller access

Features: Play equipment for tots (see below), restrooms, changing table, food and drink in vending machines

No nursing privacy

The City of Renton has provided well for this community center, which is filled with kids in classes for children under three. Although there is no drop-in activity, you can register your newborn, infant or toddler for a number of different offerings. Also, there is a preschool called Almost 3's Preschool that is designed for youngsters who are about to turn three.

Kindermusik Village. This Kindermusik class provides musical stimulation for newborns, infants and toddlers. The session meets for forty-five minutes once a week.

Terrific Tots Playground. This is an indoor playground that meets three days a week for an hour and a half. You can sign up for one, two or all three days a week. Parents must stay with their child, but the center provides the toys.

Messy Time for 2's. Two-year-olds can express themselves with various art mediums for forty-five minutes once a week. Parents stay with their children.

Parent/Infant Class. A nurse teaches parents about infant development and more. Parents take their baby to this ninety-minute class.

Toddlersize. For forty-five minutes once a week, toddlers and their parents or nannies can participate in group activities for playing and learning.

SAMENA SWIM and RECREATION CLUB

www.samena.com

(425) 746–1160
15231 Lake Hills Boulevard, Bellevue

Hours and fees: Monday–Friday 5 a.m.–10 p.m., Saturday 7 a.m.–10 p.m., Sunday 9 a.m.–10 p.m.; call for class times and fees and times that childcare is available

Classes: Kindermusik Beginnings (18 months–31/2 years); Kindermusik Villages (0–18 months); Childcare (Infants–8 years)

Weekend/evening hours: Nothing available for tots

Access: Parking; stroller access

Features: Play equipment for tots (in play area), restrooms, food and drink

No nursing privacy

This fitness and swim club has been serving the Eastside for forty years. Members enjoy a full range of activities. In addition to swimming and fitness equipment, the club offers dance, yoga, aerobic classes and more. Their many classes, including those for infants and toddlers, are open to both members and non-members.

Kindermusik Beginnings. Once a week children and their caregivers meet for a half-hour of musical fun. Children are encouraged to explore music through singing, dancing and playing musical instruments.

Kindermusik Villages. This class, which introduces music to young children, is specifically for infants with their parents.

SWIMMING POOLS: Tot Swim

Bellevue Aquatics Center, Issaqah's Julius Boehm Pool, Peter Kirk Pool, Redmond City Pool, Bellevue Family YMCA, Water-babies Aquatic Program; see Multiple Locations, pages 29–31.

VILLAGE THEATRE

www.villagetheatre.org

(425) 392–2202
303 Front Street N, Issaquah

Hours and fees: Box office is open Tuesday–Saturday 11 a.m.–7 p.m. Call for shows, times and fees.

Weekend/evening hours: Yes

Access: Parking; stroller access

Features: Restrooms, food and drink in café next door, nursing privacy

No play equipment for tots, no changing table

This Issaquah theater features live family productions. The theater's two family rooms are strategically located for fine viewing. These soundproof rooms are less expensive than the regular seating. You'll find it's a great way to attend the theater with your infant without worrying about feeding or possible crying.

WOODINVILLE COMMUNITY CENTER/CAROL EDWARDS CENTER

www.ci.woodinville.wa.us

(425) 398-9327
17401 133rd Avenue NE, Woodinviille

Hours and fees: Monday, Friday 9 a.m.–5 p.m., Tuesday—Thursday 9 a.m.–9 p.m., Saturday 9 a.m.–noon; call for seasonal classes, times and fees

Weekend/evening hours: Yes

Access: Parking; stroller access

Features: Restrooms, food and drink in vending machines

No changing table, no nursing privacy

Classes: Indoor Playground (18 months–4 years) $2 per child

 The Indoor Playground at the Woodinville Community Center is located in their gym, which makes things feel spacious, even when the playground is busy. There are balls, climbing toys, scooters, games and lots of toys to keep your little one busy for several hours. The center closes the Indoor Playground during the summer months.

South Snohomish County

As the affordability of living in the city of Seattle becomes more challenging, the areas of Edmonds, Lynnwood, Mountlake Terrace and Mill Creek are becoming more and more populated. Close to Seattle, but far enough out to feel as if you're living in the suburbs, these cities offer local activities to parents not in the mood to fight traffic in order to find something for their child to do.

ANDERSON CENTER

www.ci.edmonds.wa.us

(425) 771-0230
700 Main Street, Edmonds

Hours and fees: Monday-Friday 8 a.m.–10 p.m., Saturday 9 a.m.–5 p.m.; call for class times and fees

Access: Parking; stroller access

Classes: Signing With Your Baby (7 months and up); Wiggles & Giggles (6 months–2 years); Fun Factory (1–5 years); Mini Me Fun Factory (12–30 months); Mommy/Daddy & Me Soccer (2–3½ years)

Weekend/evening hours: Yes for Signing With Your Baby

Features: Restrooms, food and drink nearby, nursing privacy

The Anderson Center houses most of the Edmonds community classes. Although it does not have a drop-in play area, the center is located right next to a small park, which has a climbing structure that is suitable for experienced walkers.

Signing With Your Baby: Founded on the text, "Sign With Your Baby" by Joseph Garcia, this class will teach you vocabulary and techniques to help you communicate with your baby. Babies are welcome or adults may attend without their child.

Wiggles and Giggles: This class starts with songs and includes parachute play, music and bubbles for forty-five minutes. The instructor also provides weekly information on things to do with your toddler or recipes your child might enjoy.

Fun Factory: This is a hands-on, messy, fun class that experiments with paints, dough, sand, water, noise, art and action. This is a loosely structured class that allows time to make new friends and focus on large motor skills.

Mini Me Fun Factory: A scaled down version of the Fun Factory geared toward the younger ones.

Mommy/Daddy & Me Soccer: In this class, you don't watch the instruction from the sidelines – you get to be right out there with your child while they learn social and motor skills that center around soccer.

FUNTASIA FAMILY FUN CENTER

www.familyfunpark.com

(425) 775-2174

7212 220th Street SW, Edmonds

Hours and fees: Sunday-Thursday 11 a.m.–10:30 p.m., Friday 11 a.m.–11:30 p.m., Saturday 10 a.m.–11:30 p.m. Admission is free, games and attractions priced individually

Access: Parking; stroller access

Weekend/evening hours: Yes

Features: Restrooms, food and drink

No changing table, no nursing privacy

Most of the activities at Funtasia are for older children. However, there is the Fun Fortress Playland, which will delight your walker! For $5 and an unlimited amount of time, your child may climb, slide, bounce and jump in this 4000 square foot playland. This is a great place to go if you have older children whom you'd like to keep entertained while you watch your baby.

LYNNWOOD RECREATION CENTER

www.ci.lynnwood.wa.us

(425) 771-4020

18900 44th Avenue W, Lynnwood

Hours and fees: Monday-Friday 5:30 a.m.–10 p.m., Saturday 7 a.m.–8:45 p.m., Sunday 12 p.m.–6 p.m.; call for seasonal classes, times and fees

Access: Parking; stroller access

Classes: Music 4 Preschool (2-3 years), Toddler Time Gymnastics (walkers–3 years)

Features: Restrooms, food and drink in vending machines and nearby

Weekend/evening hours: No

No changing table, no nursing privacy

Music 4 Preschool. This class explores different musical styles, from African to Jazz. You and your child will enjoy music together, through singing, playing instruments, parachute time and movement.

Toddler Time Gymnastics. In this fun atmosphere, with your help, your child will learn marching, movement, gymnastics, and swinging as they relate to the concepts of up and down, in and out, and through. Bubbles, parachutes and new activities each week help keep your child's excitement.

MILL CREEK PARKS AND RECREATION

www.cityofmillcreek.com

(425) 745-1891
Mill Creek City Hall, 15728 Main Street, Mill Creek

Hours and fees: Monday-Friday 9 a.m.–5 p.m.; call for class times and fees

Access: Parking; stroller access

Features: Restrooms, changing tables, food and drink within walking distance

Weekend/evening hours: No

Classes: Music for Preschool (18 months–3 years), Toddle Time Gymnastics (18 months–3 years), Advanced Toddle Time (2½-3½ years)

Music for Preschool. This class explores a variety of music, to include jazz, classical, reggae and rock 'n' roll. Children dance, sing and discover rhythm in a fun-filled forty-five-minute session.

Toddle Time Gymnastics. Walking, running, marching, and

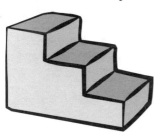

moving to music are just some of the activities in this class designed to teach the concepts of up, down, in, out and through.

Advanced Toddle Time. This is the second level of Toddle Time Gymnastics and introduces gymnastic equipment to your child.

MOUNTLAKE TERRACE COMMUNITY CENTER (AT THE RECREATION PAVILLION)

www.ci.mountlake-terrace.wa.us

(425) 776-9173
5303 228th Street SW, Mountlake Terrace

Hours and fees: Monday-Thursday 6 a.m.–9:30 p.m., Friday 6 a.m.–8 p.m., Saturday 7:30 a.m.–7:30 p.m., Sunday 9 a.m.–7:30 p.m.; call for class times and fees

Access: Parking; stroller access

Features: Restrooms, food and drink in vending machines

Weekend/evening hours: Yes

Classes: Indoor Playground (crawlers–5 years) $2.50 for residents, $3 for non-residents, Playground Pals (9 months–5 years) $2 for residents, $2.50 for non-residents, Terrific Twos (2 years), Playschool Co-op (2–4 years)

No changing table

Indoor Playground. This inviting play area has a tree house, play house, ride-on toys, balls, a crawler's corner, a ball pit, and more.

Playground Pals. Supervision is provided in the Indoor Playground for up to an hour and fifteen minutes while parents participate in a class within the Pavillion.

Terrific Twos. This class includes a half hour in the Indoor Playground, along with singing, dancing and creating projects to take home. This is a parent/child class.

Playschool Co-op. This class also includes a half hour in the Indoor Playground. Other activities include songs, dance, and arts and crafts in a more educational setting. Some parent participation is required.

PUMP IT UP

www.pumpitupparty.com

(425) 820-2297

18027 Highway 99, Suite J, Lynnwood

Hours and fees: Tuesday and Wednesday 9–11:45 a.m., $6 for first child, $4 for siblings (parents are free)

Access: Parking; stroller access

Features: Restrooms, changing tables

No nursing privacy

Pump It Up is generally reserved for parties and group activities; however, the Lynnwood facility now offers Pop-In Playtime. Both days offer two play sessions that last one hour and fifteen minutes. Available only for kids five and under, this is fun environment in which your child can burn off some energy. There are multiple recreational inflatable structures on which kids can climb, bounce, slide and tumble.

CHAPTER TWO
Bringing Out Baby
Creepers, Crawlers & Toddlers
OUTSIDE

Most of us who reside in Washington live for sunny days, and as soon as the weather is decent, we make a beeline for the outdoors. This chapter will help you choose a park or activity in which the majority of the area is outside.

Parks and playgrounds have a variety of play equipment. A slide is mentioned if it is suitable for a small child; most tunneled and curved slides are inappropriate. Only swings suitable for tots are listed. Jungle gyms are included in the climber category; unusual climbers are usually described in detail. A spinner or merry-go-round is the apparatus that a child sits or stands on while a parent spins it. A bouncer is an apparatus shaped like an animal or car, and mounted on a steel coil.

If there is a wading pool, the Wading Pool Hotline number is given; call for times and dates that the pool is open.

In playgrounds, play area surfaces are described. Sand is good for children over a year old, when they can use shovels and pails and generally no longer eat it or throw it. Gravel and pebbles can be hard for a new walker. Wood chips are the surface of choice in newer playgrounds.

Montlake, Madison Park, Capitol Hill & the Central Area

CASCADE PARK

Harrison Street and Pontius Avenue, Central

Access: Street parking; stroller access

Features: Two children's play areas, with one suitable for tots (climbers, slides), sand play area, paved walking trail, restrooms, picnic areas, some shade, nursing privacy

No changing table

This newly renovated city park is located in the heart of the Denny Triangle in downtown Seattle. It's an oasis in the middle of a sea of apartment complexes, small restaurants and businesses. Located adjacent to a p-patch community garden, this park is popular with employees of nearby office buildings and also a preschool located kitty-corner to the park.

GARFIELD COMMUNITY CENTER PARK

2323 Cherry Street E, Central

Access: Parking; stroller access

Features: Play equipment for tots (slides, swings, climbers, spinner), woodchip play area surface, restrooms, changing table, nursing privacy, food and drink in vending machines, some shade

This small playground is part of the Garfield Community Center. The play equipment may be a little sophisticated for toddlers, but the park can be used if you have been visiting the Garfield Family Center and want to take your child outside. Restrooms, changing table and vending machines are in the center.

MADISON PARK

Madison Street and 42nd Avenue E, Madison Park

Access: Parking

Features: Play equipment for tots (slides, swings, climbers, bouncers, spinner), sand play area surface, restrooms by the beach, some nursing privacy, some shade

No stroller access, no changing table

This is an exciting park to visit with children of all ages. Toddlers can be kept busy with the play equipment while infants  will enjoy picking dandelions off the grassy field. Stop first for a bagel and coffee or other beverage from a neighborhood shop. A cool breeze often blows off Lake Washington on hot summer days, so you might want sweaters for you and your child. Just east of the playground is a beach with restrooms.

POWELL BARNETT PARK

Wading pool hotline **(206) 684-7796**
352 Martin Luther King Way, Central

Access: Parking; stroller access

Features: Play equipment for tots (firehouse, house and ship), spinners, tricycle maze, picnic tables, restrooms, shade, nursing privacy

No changing table

Recently voted as one of Seattle's top parks for kids, this park has something for children of all ages. There are numerous spinners of different kinds, and the play structure for the younger ones is very inviting with its bright colors and themes. If your child has recently learned to ride a tricycle, the maze will really help them develop their riding skills.

ROANOKE PARK

Roanoke Street and Broadway E, Montlake

Access: Parking; stroller access

Features: Play equipment for tots (slides, swings, climbers), sand play area surface, some nursing privacy, some shade

No restrooms, no changing table, no food or drink

This pleasant neighborhood park lies nestled between the Highway 520 freeway and Interstate 5, making the noise factor high during rush hours. It is also right across the street from a fire station. If the noise potential does not deter you, this neighborhood is an attractive place to walk, and the park makes a nice resting spot.

VOLUNTEER PARK

Wading pool hotline **(206) 684–7796**
Prospect Street and 14th Avenue E, Capitol Hill

Access: Parking; stroller access

Features: Play equipment for tots (slides, swings, climbers, bouncers) sand play area surface, wading pool, restrooms, nursing privacy, shade

No changing table, no food or drink available

As you drive into Volunteer Park you will see a large brick water tower. Continue on, passing the Asian Art Museum and reaching the top of the park. Stop here, get out the stroller, and walk to the greenhouse conservatory. Most of the beautiful plants and flowers on display here are low enough to permit good stroller viewing.

A short walk from the Conservatory is a large playground that offers a variety of equipment. The play area and round wading pool are partially shaded. This pool is huge and is considered to be one of Seattle's "Big Three" wading pools. Across from the playground is a large grassy field where you and your baby can stretch out and relax.

WASHINGTON PARK ARBORETUM

(206) 343-8800
Lake Washington Boulevard and Madison Street E, Madison Park

Access: Parking; jog stroller access

Features: Restrooms, nursing privacy, shade

No play equipment for tots, no changing table, no food or drink available

The Washington Park Arboretum is a large botanical preserve in the middle of Seattle's Montlake District. Winding trails take you through beds of a variety of beautiful flowers, and the gift shop is a pleasant stop. Bring a pack and a lunch and take the time to enjoy this bit of nature within the big city. There is a small play area in the lower area of the park and the walk over the bridge that spans Lake Washington Boulevard is very nice.

Queen Anne

EAST QUEEN ANNE PLAYFIELD

Wading pool hotline (206) 684–7796
  1912 Warren Avenue N

Access: Parking; stroller access

Features: Play equipment for tots (swings), sand play area surface, wading pool, restrooms, some shade

No changing table, no nursing privacy, no food or drink available

This quaint neighborhood park holds a nice, slightly shaded wading pool. The playground is small, but is adequate for toddlers. This is a fine park to walk to for a short visit.

DAVID ROGERS PARK

2500 1st Avenue

Access: Parking scarce—try 3rd Avenue; stroller access

Features: Play equipment for tots (slides, swings, climbers, spinner), woodchip play area surface, restrooms, nursing privacy, shade

No changing table, no food or drink available

The city of Seattle has recently built a new playground at Rogers Park, a large wooded area on the northern slope of Queen Anne hill. Parking is tight, so the park is best for those visitors who live within walking distance. Trees provide the shade and privacy needed for mothers of very young infants.

WEST QUEEN ANNE PLAYFIELD

150 W Blaine Street

Access: Parking; stroller access

Features: Play equipment for tots (slides, swings, climbers, spinner), sand play area surface, restrooms in community center, little shade

No changing table, no food or drink available, no nursing privacy

This playground in the center of Queen Anne Hill offers play equipment appropriate for toddlers and older children. Because it is near a middle school, you might want to avoid the park during lunchtime and after school. I went when classes were in session and the playground was empty. The community center about 50 yards to the east doesn't have activities for babies, but there is a restroom in the building. Restaurants can be found on Queen Anne Boulevard, a few blocks away.

Magnolia

BAYVIEW PARK

Armour Street and 24th Avenue W

Access: Parking; stroller access

Features: Play equipment for tots (slide, swings, climbers), sand play area surface, restrooms, moderate shade

No changing table, no food or drink available, no nursing privacy

This small park is found in a quiet Magnolia neighborhood. The playground is above the playfield and is well shaded. Parking is on the streets surrounding the park.

DISCOVERY PARK

Commodore Way and 40th Avenue W

Access: Parking; stroller access

Features: Restrooms, nursing privacy, shade

No stroller access, no play equipment for tots, no changing table, no food or drink available

If you like to hike but do not want to drive out of the city, this park is for you. Trails ramble throughout the wooded preserve. One of the best trails runs through a wooded incline and along a ridge overlooking Puget Sound. Lush meadows invite resting and picnicking. Bring your back carrier because strollers will not work well on the dirt trails. Be careful if you let your toddler walk along the trail because there are some drop-off points along the bluff. Check out the visitor's center and ask about the toddler nature walks.

LAWTON PARK

Thurman Street and 26th Avenue W

Access: Parking on 26th Avenue; stroller access

Features: Play equipment for tots (slides, swings, climbers, spinner), sand play area surface, some nursing privacy, some shade

No restrooms, no changing table, no food or drink available

Terraced Lawton Park is built into the northern slope of Magnolia Bluff, overlooking Ballard. A small playground is located above Lawton School in the middle of a hilly, forested park. A paved pathway leads up to the playground, and wooded trails go deeper into the park. When parking on 26th Avenue, park by the pathway, not by the school's private playground. You may also park on Williams Avenue and take the path to the park.

MAGNOLIA PARK

Clise Place and Galer Avenue W

Access: Parking on street; stroller access

Features: Restrooms, nursing privacy, shade

No play equipment for tots, no changing table, no food or drink available

This beautiful piece of land is located on the western bluff of Magnolia. Although no play equipment is available, picnic benches are plentiful. To the west is a magnificent view of Puget Sound. Magnolia Park is easily accessed from the Magnolia Bridge.

WEST MAGNOLIA PLAYGROUND

2550 W 34th Avenue

Access: Parking; stroller access

Features: Play equipment for tots (slide, swings, climbers, spinner), sand play area surface, restrooms, food and drink on McGraw Avenue, some shade

No changing table, no nursing privacy

This very popular park has enough equipment available to keep every youngster busy, although the slides may be a bit too difficult for some toddlers to negotiate. The playground rests below the community center, preventing children from running into the street. A grassy field adjacent to the playground is perfect for the non-walking child. Restrooms and vending machines are  in the community center, but for coffee and food try McGraw Avenue.

See the Magnolia Community Center description, pages 36–37.

Green Lake, Wallingford & Ravenna

COWEN PARK

Ravenna Boulevard and 15th Avenue NE, Ravenna

Access: Parking; stroller access

Features: Play equipment for tots (slides, swings) woodchip play area surface, restrooms, nursing privacy, shade

No changing table, no food or drink available

A playground graces the southeast corner of this park. Cowen Park is actually an extension of Ravenna Park; both are situated along a wooded ravine. A smattering of picnic tables dapple the inner regions of the park where it intertwines with its sister and becomes one large play area. There is enough shade for comfort and plenty of places to bask in the warmth of an April sun. The wooded area between Cowen Park and Ravenna Park has been known to be a hangout for homeless teenagers.

GAS WORKS PARK

Northlake Way and Burke Avenue NE, Wallingford

Access: Parking; stroller access

Features: Play equipment for tots (slides, climbers, spinner), sand play area surface, restrooms, food and drink at concession stand, nursing privacy, some shade

No changing table

Gas Works Park has a gorgeous view of Lake Union and downtown Seattle. This old plant turned coal and oil into gas until 1956. The rusted old gas pipes and pumps rising out of the ground now serve as a memorial to days gone by. A covered section contains brightly painted pipes, cranks and other mechanisms. At two, my son was thrilled to just look at the "'chines." The land this park sits on is still contaminated. A sign instructs park users to wash hands after touching the grass, so I don't recommend this park for children who are not yet walking.

GREEN LAKE PARK

Wading pool hotline **(206) 684–7796**

7201 E Green Lake Drive, Green Lake

Access: Parking at parking lots around the lake; stroller access

Features: Play equipment for tots (swings, slide, spinner, climbers and other equipment), woodchip and sand play area surfaces, wading pool, restrooms, changing table in community center, some nursing privacy, some shade (no shade over playground)

Green Lake Park is one of the most popular destinations in

Seattle. A rebuilt, three-mile long pathway that circles the lake provides wonderful exercise for walkers, runners, skaters and strollers. All around the lake are areas for picnicking and sunbathing. A large wading pool on the north side of the lake teems with children in the summertime. Soccer, softball and volleyball games fill up the playfield on the southeast corner.

During weekends and evenings the park is crowded, but the

path is large enough for everyone. The popular playground by the community center has the standard equipment along with some unique pull toys that older toddlers find exciting. Keep in mind, this playground is almost always crowded and can be overwhelming for small children.

See the Green Lake Community Center description, pages 48-49.

MERIDIAN PARK

50th Street and Meridian Avenue NE, Green Lake

Access: Parking; stroller access

Features: Play equipment for tots (swings, slide, climbers), sand play area surface, restrooms, nursing privacy, some shade

No changing table, no food or drink available

Enclosed in a fortress-like wall are the Good Shepherd Center and Meridian Park, a large grassy play site. The playground has play equipment suitable for tots. The sand area is especially fun as kids can turn on a waterspout to create a river. A grade school uses this park during recess, so it can be busy during school hours.

RAVENNA PARK

Wading pool hotline (206) 684–7796

Ravenna Boulevard and 21st Avenue NE, Ravenna

Access: Parking; no stroller access

Features: Play equipment for tots (slides, swings, climbers), sand play area surface, wading pool, restrooms, nursing privacy, shade

No changing table, no food or drink available

Ravenna Park is larger than it looks at first glance. The playground is small, but just up a path the park curves toward the west and provides a secluded area with picnic benches and a quiet grassy knoll to lie on and relax. The wading pool, located up from the playground, is little but warms up quickly in the sun. Despite the playground's diminutive size, it is a very popular place all year long.

WALLINGFORD PARK

Wading pool hotline (206) 684–7796
43rd Street and Woodlawn Avenue NE, Wallingford

Access: Parking; stroller access

Features: Play equipment for tots (slides, swings, climbers, spinner), sand play area surface, wading pool, restrooms (closed in winter), some shade

No changing table, no food or drink available, no nursing privacy

This park in the Wallingford district is both entertaining and popular. The playground is located next to a large meadow that

is ideal for picnics or just lying around. Seven slides, as well as tot swings, regular swings and a tire, provide amusement for youngsters of all ages. The wading pool is not shaded or near grass. I brought my baby here before he could crawl and after he could walk and he enjoyed himself both times. Wallingford Center is a short walk northeast on 45th Avenue. There you can shop for food, drink, clothes and games for yourself and your baby.

Haller Lake, Northgate, Bitter Lake & Lake City

BITTER LAKE PARK

Wading pool hotline (206) 684–7796
Linden Avenue and 130th Avenue N, Bitter Lake

Access: Parking; stroller access

Features: Play equipment for tots (slides, swings, bouncer, spinner), woodchip play area surface, wading pool, restrooms, changing table in community center, food and drink in community center vending machines and on Aurora Avenue, shade

No nursing privacy

A recently renovated playground on the southeast corner of

Bitter Lake Park sports climbers for all skill levels, bouncers, swings and a wading pool. A sandbox of sorts is available for digging when your little one wants to take a break from running around. A paved pathway parallels the Bitter Lake shore a safe distance from the water. The great numbers of ducks and geese that have found this lake will make it interesting for your little one.

See the Bitter Lake Community Center description, pages 45-46.

DAHL PLAYGROUND

Wading pool hotline **(206) 684–7796**
80th Street and 25th Avenue NE, Lake City

Access: Parking; stroller access

Features: Play equipment for tots (slides, swings, climbers, spinner), sand play area surface, wading pool, restrooms, minimal shade

No changing table, no food or drink available, no nursing privacy

Dahl Playground borders busy 25th Avenue, so the park is noisy. However, because it is above the street, it is a bit removed from traffic. Interesting play equipment and a wading pool are not well shaded. This is a park for walkers who do not mind lathering up with sunscreen.

LAKE CITY PARK

123rd Street and 26th Avenue NE, Lake City

Access: Parking; stroller access

Features: Play equipment for tots (slides, bouncer, climbers, spinner), sand play area surface, some nursing privacy, some shade

No restrooms, no changing table, no food or drink available

Play equipment is available to keep baby busy in this quaint park. Paved pathways that meander around the sheared lawn give a feeling of a city park within a residential area. The equipment is old but still in good shape. The major downside to this park is the lack of shade and restrooms.

LICHTON SPRINGS PARK

97th Street and Ashworth Avenue NE, Northgate

Access: Parking; stroller access

Features: Play equipment for tots (slides, swings, climbers) woodchip play area surface, restrooms, food and drink at Oak Tree Village (six blocks away), some nursing privacy, some shade

No changing table

This historic park is built around Lichton Springs, which were discovered in 1870. On the northwest side of the park is a new

playground with colorful climbers and other apparatus to play on. The play-lot is not shaded, but you can find shade nearby. A partially paved walkway leads through the park and down to the springs. A quick drive will take you to Oak Tree Village where Larry's Market is one of the places you will be able to find something to eat.

MAPLE LEAF PARK

83rd Street and Roosevelt Way NE, Lake City

Access: Parking; stroller access

Features: Play equipment for tots (slides, swings, climbers, spinner, bouncer), sand play area surface, restrooms

No changing table, no food or drink available, no nursing privacy, no shade

Although there is no shade and the play-lot is just above Roosevelt Way, this is a very popular park. The playground sits between the reservoir to the east and a busy street to the west. A small field next to the lot is also unshaded.

MATTHEWS BEACH

93rd Street and Sand Point Way NE, North Seattle

Access: Parking; no stroller access

Features: Play equipment for tots (slides, swings, climbers), sand play area surface, restrooms, nursing privacy, shade

No changing table, no food or drink available

Matthews Beach, which lies on the shore of Lake Washington, is both a large park and a beach. The beach is a sliver of sand; so most sunbathing is done on the grass. The playground looks impressive, but may be too challenging for younger toddlers. There are two ways to get to this park. The hard, but fun way is to ride your bike up the Burke-Gilman Trail, with your child in a carrier, until you reach the beach turn off. The easier way is to drive and leave your car in the spacious parking lot.

NORTH ACRES PARK

Wading pool hotline **(206) 684–7796**
  130th Street and 1st Avenue NE, Haller Lake

Access: Parking; stroller access

Features: Play equipment for tots (slides, swings climbers), sand play area surface, wading pool, nursing privacy, shade

No restrooms, no changing table, no food or drink available

This shady park has ample grass and woods and a playground with a large sandbox and wading pool. The park also has dirt trails for a jogging stroller or backpack hike, but is dark and a bit rundown. Because it is well shaded, the sand tends to stay wet.

RICHMOND BEACH

190th Street and 20th Avenue NW, Shoreline

Access: Parking; stroller access up to the sand

Features: Play equipment for tots (slides, swings, climbers), sand play area surface, restrooms, nursing privacy

No changing table, no food or drink available, no shade

At Richmond Beach the parking area is above the beach, and the playground is above the parking lot. A paved path to the

beach leads over train tracks to the Sound. However, once at the beach, it is impossible to push your stroller on the sand. The covered picnic area is the only place where you will find shade. This is a fine beach for sunbathing, playing in the sand or swimming in the cold water of Puget Sound.

SACAJAWEA PLAYGROUND

94th Street and 15th Avenue NE, Lake City

Access: Parking; no stroller access

Features: Play equipment for tots (slides, tire, swings, climbers) sand play area surface, nursing privacy, shade

No restrooms, no changing table, no food or drink available

This playground built into a hillside is easy to miss. When driving on NE 94th Street you will first see a field. Just to the west of this field is the play area. A grade school to the north is not near enough to cause any distractions to park visitors. If you live in the area, you will want to visit this park.

VICTORY HEIGHTS PLAYGROUND

105th Street and 19th Avenue NE, Lake City

Access: Parking; stroller access

Features: Play equipment for tots (slides, swings, climbers, spinner) pebble play area surface, restrooms, little shade

No changing table, no food or drink available, no nursing privacy

A small preschool next to this neighborhood park could cause competition for the equipment if the school children are out playing. Other than that, this adequate playground and park is suitable for you and your baby.

Laurelhurst & View Ridge

LAURELHURST PLAYGROUND

41st Street and 46th Avenue NE, Laurelhurst

Access: Parking; stroller access

Features: Play equipment for tots (slides, swings, climbers, spinner), sand play area surface, restrooms, nursing privacy, partial shade

No changing table, no food or drink available

This excellent neighborhood park provides plenty of activity for toddlers. The playground has a variety of equipment for a whole range of ages. There also are open fields for romping or just relaxing. The community center is small, but has a restroom in the basement. Some of the grass and a little of the playground are shaded so your infant can be protected from the sun while your toddler plays on the apparatus.

BRYANT PARK

65th Street and 40th Avenue NE, View Ridge

Access: Parking; stroller access

Features: Play equipment for tots (slides, swings, climbers, spinner, bouncer), woodchip play area surface, food and drink at Puget Consumers Co-op on 65th Street, nursing privacy, some shade

No restrooms, no changing table

This refurbished playground has fresh wood shavings on the play surface instead of dirty sand. Two pieces of climbing equipment have slides; one is appropriate for toddlers. Puget Consumers Co-op market is right across the street so it's easy to get lunch at their deli or pick up some last-minute items for dinner.

BURKE-GILMAN PLACE PARK

5200 NE Sandpoint Way, Laurelhurst

Access: Parking; stroller access

Features: Play equipment for tots (slides, swings, climbers), woodchip play area surface, restrooms

No changing table, no food or drink available, no nursing privacy, no shade

Located off the Burke-Gilman Trail, this playground offers a pleasant break to a bicycling parent whose toddler has been riding in a bike trailer for a while. The playground, rebuilt in the spring of 1999, offers the standard equipment for burning off energy. It is next to a daycare so expect to share the grounds with a group of youngsters on sunny weekdays.

BURKE-GILMAN TRAIL

Main Access Points: Gas Works Park, Ravenna Boulevard and 25th Avenue NE, Matthews Beach, Tracy Owen Station

Access: Parking; stroller access

Features: Play equipment for tots (see Burke-Gilman Place Park and Matthews Beach), restrooms, shade along the trail

No changing table, no food or drink available, no nursing privacy

The Burke-Gilman Trail was a railroad right-of-way bordering Lake Union and Lake Washington between Gas Works Park and Tracy Owen Station in Kenmore. In 1978 the original 12.1 miles of track were paved over to make a wonderful bike, stroller and walking path. As additional right-of-way has been acquired, the trail has been extended, and it now starts in Ballard. At Redmond's Blyth Park, the Burke-Gilman Trail becomes the Sammamish River Trail, which leads into Marymoor Park in Redmond. If you start at Gas Works Park you will travel over twenty miles to Marymoor Park. There are access points along the path. Burke-Gilman Place Park and Matthews Beach are both accessible from the trail and provide your toddler respite from sitting in a bike trailer.

MAGNUSON PARK

Wading pool hotline **(206) 684–7796**
  65th Street and Sandpoint Way NE, View Ridge

Access: Parking; stroller access

Features: Play equipment for tots (slides, swings, climbers, bouncers), woodchip play area surface, wading pool, restrooms, nursing privacy, some shade

No changing table, no food or drink available

This large playground is located at the north end of Magnuson Park. Filled with colorful climbers, it is most easily reached via the Naval Station Puget Sound. Don't be intimidated by the manned booth; just tell the officer you want to go to the playground and he will direct you. The waterfront offers swimming in Lake Washington and a large grassy field provides a place for kite flying. There is also an off-leash area for your dog.

VIEW RIDGE PARK

Wading pool hotline **(206) 684–7796**
  70th Street and 45th Avenue NE, View Ridge

Access: Parking on 45th Avenue; stroller access

Features: Play equipment for tots (slides, swings, climbers, spinner), sand play area surface, wading pool, restrooms, some shade

No changing table, no food or drink available, no nursing privacy

Two separate playgrounds 50 yards apart make up this park. The restrooms and wading pool are in the middle and a large playfield borders both playgrounds on the north. Head for the tot playground on the southwest corner. Unfortunately, parking is available only on 45th Avenue on the east side of the park. Although 70th Street is a large street, it is not too noisy.

Ballard, Fremont & Phinney Ridge

BALLARD COMMUNITY CENTER PLAYGROUND

6020 NW 28th Avenue, Ballard

Access: Parking; stroller access

Features: Play equipment for tots (slides, swings, climbers, spinner), sand play area surface, restrooms, food and drink in vending machines, some shade

No changing table, no nursing privacy

This small playground by the Ballard Community Center has a nautical theme. Easily negotiated climbers and slides located on sand are fun for youngsters. Restrooms and vending machines are in the center.

See the Ballard Community Center description, page 42.

CARKEEK PARK

110th Street and Carkeek Park Road NW, Ballard

Access: Parking; no stroller access

Features: Play equipment for tots (slides, bouncers), pebble play area surface, restrooms, nursing privacy, some shade

No changing table, no food or drink available

This large preserve on Puget Sound has a spectacular view of the Olympic Mountains. To get to the beach, which is below the parking lot, you must walk down a large flight of steps, so the park is not stroller accessible. The creative design of the playground imitates a fish stream, and has a large salmon-shaped tube slide. The slide is difficult for a small toddler to navigate so I cannot recommend it for unstable walkers. Hiking trails are plentiful; put your baby in a backpack and take a walk.

GILMAN PARK

Wading pool hotline **(206) 684–7796**
54th Street and 11th Avenue NW, Ballard

Access: Parking; stroller access

Features: Play equipment for tots (slides, swings, spinner, low basketball hoop), sand play area surface, wading pool, restrooms, shade

No changing table, no food or drink available, no nursing privacy
This neighborhood park is crowded with older kids on weekends but is quiet during the week. The shaded wading pool is perfect for hot summer days. The park is near an industrial area to the west, but this doesn't affect the park's atmosphere.

GOLDEN GARDENS PARK

80th Street and Seaview Avenue NW, Ballard

Access: Parking; stroller access

Features: Play equipment for tots (slides, swings, climbers), sand play area surface, restrooms, food and drink in summer, nursing privacy, some shade

No changing table

Founded in 1929, historic Golden Gardens Park boasts a small playground and a meandering nature walk. The beach affords a beautiful view of the Olympic Mountains. Your little one will enjoy romping on a soft grassy meadow or playing in a shallow creek. The sandy beach provides swimming in cold Puget Sound waters.

ROSS PARK

43rd Street and 3rd Avenue NW, Fremont

Access: Parking; stroller access

Features: Play equipment for tots (slides, swings, climbers, spinner), sand play area surface, restrooms, food and drink in mini-market across the street, little nursing privacy, some shade

No changing table

Although it doesn't look like much because of its older play equipment, Ross Park provides everything needed for a toddler's fun time. Plenty of shade covers one sandy portion of the playground. There is a restroom and picnic bench. A mini-market across the street is convenient for snacks and drinks.

WEBSTER PARK

3100 NW 68th Street, Ballard

Access: Parking; stroller access

Features: Play equipment for tots (slides, swings, climbers), sand play area surface, portable outhouse

No changing table, no food or drink available, no nursing privacy, no shade

Popular Webster Park is located in front of Ballard's Nordic Heritage Museum. Toddlers and babies abound on the colorful climbers during the morning hours. Next to the playground is a large paved area with a basketball court. This can be used for rolling or running toys. The only restroom is a portable outhouse, but this doesn't seem to deter local parents from visiting this playground.

WOODLAND PARK PLAYGROUND

Phinney Ridge and 59th Street N, Phinney Ridge

Access: Parking on street, not in zoo lot; stroller access

Features: Play equipment for tots (slides, swings, climbers, bouncer), sand play area surface, food and drink at 7/11 on Phinney Avenue, some nursing privacy, some shade, but none over playground

No restrooms, no changing table

After opening in June of 1997, this new playground at Woodland Park quickly became very popular. One piece of climbing equipment is especially tot friendly, since it is low to the ground and has wide slides. The park is on the north end of the zoo and is worth a special visit. If your baby does well in a restaurant, go to the Santa Fe Café next to the 7/11. The atmosphere is surprisingly child friendly. If your baby doesn't do so well, have your spouse take her to the playground while you enjoy a nice meal.

WOODLAND PARK ZOO

www.zoo.org

(206)684-4800

601 N 59th Street, Phinney Ridge

Hours: Open 365 days per year: March 15-April 30 9:30 a.m.–5 p.m., May 1-September 14 9:30 a.m.–6 p.m., September 15-October 14 9:30 a.m.–5 p.m., October 15-March 14 9:30 a.m.–4 p.m.

Fees: Adults 13–64 $10.50; Child 3-12 $7.50; 2 and under free; seniors and those with disabilities receive a $2 discount from regular admission prices. Annual family memberships start at $70.

Access: Parking in lot ($4.00), free street parking, stroller access except in the "Night and Day" and "Rainforest" exhibits

Features: Zoomazium (see description below), play equipment for tots (slides, climbers, in the center of the zoo grounds), restrooms, changing tables in most restrooms, food and drink in large food court, nursing privacy on patches of grass in remote areas, shade

At the Woodland Park Zoo, the animals are kept in large open habitats quite like their natural environments. Sometimes this hinders viewing, since the animals have a wide area to roam, but it presents a more humane atmosphere to a child. Both paved and unpaved paths meander throughout the zoo giving visitors exceptional peeks into the lives of the various animals. A farm area with a petting zoo offers children a chance to touch tame animals such as goats and sheep. Near the family farm is a play area with things for children to play on and climb over.

Zoomazium is an indoor/outdoor nature play space right in the middle of the zoo grounds. Offering a safe environment to explore nature and animals, Zoomazium is the perfect place to allow your toddler to run around

and have hands-on fun before exploring the zoo. There is a tree trunk to climb through, a manmade rock climbing structure, a small aquarium, and plush toys in an enclosed play space designated just for toddlers. If you also have older children, they will enjoy climbing the 20-foot tree or crossing a rope bridge nestled within a tree canopy.

Crown Hill & Loyal Heights

LOYAL HEIGHTS PLAYGROUND

2101 NW 77th Street, Loyal Heights

Access: Parking; stroller access

Features: Play equipment for tots (slides, swings, climbers, bouncers), woodchip play area surface, restrooms, changing table

No food or drink available, no nursing privacy, no shade   Ballard, Fremont & Phinney Ridge

This tot-lot sports colorful and creative equipment. Bring plenty of sunscreen because there is not much shade. Inside the community center you will find restrooms and indoor activities.
See the Loyal Heights Community Center description, pages 50–51.

SALMON BAY PARK

Sloop Place and 19th Avenue NW, Loyal Heights

Access: Parking; stroller access

Features: Play equipment for tots (slides, swings, climbers, spinner, bouncer), sand play area surface, restrooms, shade

No changing table, no food or drink available, no nursing privacy

The equipment at Salmon Bay Park is bright and colorful. A paved pathway that cuts through rolling woods provides stroller access to the playground at the southeast corner. The restroom is a good distance from the playground, which is inconvenient.

SANDEL PLAYGROUND

Wading pool hotline **(206) 684–7796**
92nd Street and 1st Avenue NW, Crown Hill

Access: Parking; stroller access

Features: Play equipment for tots (slides, swings, climbers), sand play area surface, wading pool, restrooms, some nursing privacy, some shade

No changing table, no food or drink available

This small playground reminds me of a little cove surrounded by grass and trees. Because the park is below an incline, you cannot see the street from the playground. A pathway loops around the large playfield next to the site.

Shoreline

PARAMOUNT PARK

152nd Street and 10th Avenue NE

Access: Parking; stroller access

Features: Play equipment for tots (slides, climbers), woodchip play area surface

No restrooms, no changing table, no food or drink available, no nursing privacy, no shade

Paramount Park is ideal for joggers who need a smooth track to run with a jog stroller. A paved walkway about the half the length of a football field loops around a large field and playground. There is no shade, so take plenty of sunscreen. The play-lot is not suitable for babies since it lacks a sandbox and tot swing.

Mercer Island

DEANE'S CHILDREN'S PARK

5500 Island Crest Way, Mercer Island

Access: Parking; stroller access

Features: Tot play structure (slides), sit-on sand digger, stand-alone climbing boulder, restrooms, shade, nursing privacy

No changing table

Also known as Dragon Park because of the big concrete dragon in the middle of the park, this park has undergone a renovation that has made it much more appealing to children of all ages. The tot play structure has a castle theme and includes a seesaw, drum and metallophone. The old metal climbing dome that's still present may invite you to join in with your child and revisit your playground days.

I–90 "LID" PARK

23rd Avenue and Atlantic Street S, Mercer Island

Access: Parking; stroller access

Features: Play equipment for tots (slides, climbers, bouncers), woodchip play area surface, restrooms, nursing privacy

No changing table, no food or drink available, no shade

This large park with plenty of open space and a small sunny playground lies atop the I–90 freeway. The playground and parking lot are located close to the freeway ramps, which makes it convenient to access. It's definitely a great park for those who live on Mercer Island.

ISLAND CREST PARK

58th Street and Island Crest Way SE

Access: Parking; stroller access

Features: Play equipment for tots (slides, swings, climbers), woodchip play area surface, restrooms, nursing privacy, shade

No changing table, no food or drink available

The playground at Island Crest Park is in a wooded cove located on the north side of this large park. Hiking trails are available for backpackers. A large portion of the grounds is allocated to playfields.

LUTHER BURBANK PARK

2040 SE 84th Avenue, Mercer Island

Play equipment for tots (slides, swings, climbers), pebble play area surface, restrooms, food and drink in vending machine, nursing privacy, some shade, but none over playground

No changing table

This expansive Mercer Island park sits on the shores of Lake Washington. Walking trails interweave the meadows and restoration projects for easy hikes. The playground is an extensive web of climbing structures and slides that may be too daunting for crawlers or new walkers. Some of the apparatuses are quite high, so it may be difficult for you to sit and watch your toddler make this park a hands-on play experience. The beach lies below the park. Plenty of shade and grass are provided for picnicking and relaxing.

Mount Baker, Rainier Valley & Madrona

BRIGHTON PLAYGROUND

Juneau Street and 39th Avenue S, Rainier Valley

Access: Parking; some stroller access

Features: Play equipment for tots (slides, swings, climbers, spinner), sand play area surface, restrooms, nursing privacy, shade

No changing table, no food or drink available

This large park stretches over five city blocks. The southwest corner hosts an adequate playground that will entertain your toddler. The climbers are a little advanced so you will have to stand near to give your tot a hand. A playfield probably used by the high school borders the park on the south side.

DEARBORN PARK

Brandon Street and 29th Avenue S, Rainier Valley

Access: Parking minimal; stroller access

Features: Play equipment for tots (slides, swings, climbers), woodchip play area surface, nursing privacy, shade

No restrooms, no changing table, no food or drink available

Located above the street, this small playground is quiet and peaceful. Trees provide plenty of shade on sunny days.

MADRONA PARK

900 East Lake Washington Boulevard, Madrona

Access: No parking; stroller access

Features: Restrooms, nursing privacy, shade

No play equipment for tots, no changing table, no food or drink available

This lakefront park affords a beautiful view of Lake Washington and Mercer Island. A beach and a walkway provide a pleasant area to take a stroller. Younger infants may enjoy the beach while crawlers can play on the lush grass. However, keep a close eye as toddlers may find busy Lake Washington Boulevard, which borders the park, a dangerous attraction.

MOUNT BAKER PARK

Lake Washington Boulevard and Lake Park Drive S, Mount Baker

Access: Parking by lake; stroller access

Features: Play equipment for tots (slides, swings, climbers, bouncers), sand play area surface, restrooms, a little shade

No changing table, no food or drink available, no nursing privacy

Mount Baker Park begins by the lake and continues upward along Lake Park Drive to McClellan Avenue. Parking is available by the beach where there are grassy areas and a nice view of Mercer Island. Get your stroller out and take the wooded path up to the highest part of the park. After walking past a pretty Japanese garden you will come to a large playground.

OTHELLO PLAYGROUND

Othello Street and 45th Avenue S, Rainier Valley

Access: Parking; stroller access

Features: Play equipment for tots (slides, swings, climbers), pebble play area surface, restrooms, nursing privacy, shade

No changing table, no food or drink available

Beautiful old trees shade quiet areas of this park. Paved pathways interweave throughout the sloping grassy hills. The playground on the northeast corner is brimming with new climbing equipment appropriate for toddlers. A super-slide for older children on the playground's northwest corner is so long that it resembles an amusement park ride.

PRITCHARD BEACH

Gratten Street and Seward Park Avenue S, Rainier Valley

Access: Parking; stroller access

Features: Restrooms, nursing privacy, shade

No play equipment for tots, no changing table, no food or drink available

A sloping lawn leads to a sliver of sandy beach that drops into the water. The dip into the water is gradual, making it safer for toddlers. Few trees are available to provide shade so use of sunscreen is advised.

SEWARD PARK

Lake Washington Boulevard South and Orcas Street, Rainier Valley

Access: Parking; stroller access

Features: Play equipment for tots (slides, swings, climbers, bouncers), sand play area surface, restrooms, nursing privacy, shade

No changing table, no food or drink available

This 300-acre peninsula park offers splendid views of Lake Washington. The small tot-lot is as popular as the trails and picnic areas. Much of the area is wooded, and dirt paths wind through the trees. There is considerable activity on sunny days but you can still find areas of quiet. Parking can be tight on a sunny weekend because this is a popular destination.

West Seattle

ALKI BEACH

Alki Beach Road SW, West Seattle

Access: Parking is tight; stroller access

Features: Restrooms, food and drink, some shade

No play equipment for tots, no changing table, no nursing privacy

Sunset magazine rates this Puget Sound attraction as one of Washington's top ten beaches. Sand, grass and a walkway make up this sunny destination. Eating establishments line the street across from the beach. As the beach heads south along the walkway, it is replaced by a sea wall. This is a windy beach with a northwestern exposure, so bundle up if you are heading there on a day that is not warm and sunny.

ALKI PLAYGROUND

Lander Street and 59th Avenue SW

Access: Parking; stroller access

Features: Play equipment for tots (slides, climbers), woodchip play area surface, restrooms

No changing table, no food or drink available, no nursing privacy, no shade

This small play-lot was recently refurbished. The equipment is interesting, but there are no swings. Bring sunscreen because the play-lot has no shade.

DELRIDGE PARK

Wading pool hotline (206) 684–7796
Alaska Street and Delridge Way SW

Access: Parking; stroller access

Features: Play equipment for tots (slides, swings, climbers, spinner), woodchip play area surface, wading pool, restrooms, changing table, food and drink in vending machines, some nursing privacy, some shade

Delridge Park is a small playground located outside the community center, next to a field. The climbers and slide are difficult for toddlers to use unassisted. The wading pool is a few yards north of the playground. The changing table and vending machines are in the community center. The Delridge Community Center, which offers one of the best open gyms in Seattle, is described on page 61.

HIAWATHA PLAYGROUND

Wading pool hotline (206) 684–7796
Lander Street and California Avenue SW

Access: Parking; no stroller access

Features: Play equipment for tots (slides, swings, climbers, bouncer), woodchip play area surface, wading pool, restrooms, food and drink nearby at Puget Consumers Co-op and McDonalds, nursing privacy, shade

No changing table

This multipurpose park has a brand new playground. Tennis courts, playfields and a community center make this a popular destination in West Seattle. The playground is in the middle of a shaded grove, which helps keep things cool on hot summer days. The wading pool is a bit far from the playground.

HIGHLAND PARK

Wading pool hotline (206) 684–7796
Trenton Street and 11th Avenue SW

Access: Parking; stroller access

Features: Play equipment for tots (swings, climbers), sand and wood chipplay area surfaces, wading pool, restrooms (closed in winter), minimal shade

No changing table, no food or drink available, no nursing privacy

Highland Park is primarily for older children. However, its two separate playgrounds do have some attractions for toddlers. The first play area is situated in a large playfield. It has swings and climbers on sand and an unshaded wading pool. The second playground, which is next to the elementary school, has additional equipment with wood chips underneath.

LAKEWOOD PARK

110th Street and 10th Avenue SW

Access: Parking; stroller access

Features: Play equipment for tots (slides, swings, climbers), sand play area surface, restrooms, little nursing privacy, shade

No changing table, no food or drink available

This picturesque park wraps around a small lake. A paved pathway leads around the lake and through a meadow. Two separate play areas are available to explore. This is a pretty setting for an afternoon break.

LINCOLN PARK

Wading pool hotline (206) 684–7796
8400 SW Fauntleroy Way

Access: Parking; jog stroller access

Features: Play equipment for tots (slides, swings, climbers, bouncer), woodchip play area surface, wading pool, restrooms, nursing privacy, shade

No changing table, no food or drink available

This magnificent multipurpose park, lying on the shores of Puget Sound, hosts many family and group picnics. Dirt trails interweave throughout the woods, making standard strollers difficult to roll. The playground located in the northern portion of the park is actually two separate play areas plus a kidney-shaped wading pool. The first play area contains climbers for children of any age. The other tot-sized area boasts convenient nearby picnic benches. Trees shade many areas of the park, so you can stay out of the sun if you wish. This is a popular destination, so arrive early if you're planning a visit on a sunny weekend.

RIVERVIEW PLAYFIELD

Othello Street and 12th Avenue SW

Access: Parking; stroller access

Features: Play equipment for tots (slides, swings, climbers), sand play area surface, restrooms at south end of park, some shade

No changing table, no food or drink available, no nursing privacy

A large two-block playfield leaves space for a small playground in the northern section of this multipurpose park. Residences lining 12th Avenue make this a quiet street.

SEACREST PARK

1900 SW Seacrest Park

Access: Parking; stroller access

Features: Restrooms, food and drink across the street

No play equipment for tots, no changing table, no nursing privacy, no shade

A paved walkway that runs along the east side of West Seattle, overlooking Elliot Bay, is suitable for all types of strollers. Seacrest Park can be windy because it borders the Sound; however, it is popular spot the entire year. Find food at restaurants and delis across the street, or take the path to a grassy area with picnic tables. Farther north, the path eventually turns into a walkway along the road that

borders the sea wall. If you have an active walker you may want to avoid this park because it is so close to the water.

Bellevue & Medina

ARDMORE PARK

30th Street and 168th Place NE, Bellevue

Access: Parking on street; no stroller access

Features: Play equipment for tots (slides, swings, climbers, bouncers), woodchip play area surface, nursing privacy, shade

No restrooms, no changing table, no food or drink available

At Ardmore Park, a small forest of tall evergreen trees to the south of the playground provides morning shade on sunny days and offers trails for hiking with baby in a backpack. The playground boasts newer play equipment and an open field graces the park's west side.

BOVEE PARK

1500 NE 108th Avenue, Bellevue

Access: Parking; stroller access (gravel path)

Features: Play equipment for tots (slides, swings, climbers, bouncers), woodchip play area surface, restrooms (closed off-season), nursing privacy, shade

No changing table, no food or drink available

A wide gravel path passes by a quiet, shady plat, and then leads to a small playground. With plenty of shade and restrooms close by, the spot is perfect for small gatherings of caregivers and their babies. The slides in the playground, which are accessed by rope ladders, could be too difficult for new walkers; however, the bouncers and swings will entertain toddlers of any skill level.

CITY OF BELLEVUE DOWNTOWN PARK

4th Street and 100th Avenue NE, Bellevue

Access: Parking; stroller access

Features: Play equipment for tots (slides, swings, climbers, bouncers), woodchip play area surface, restrooms (including a tot-size restroom), picnic tables, some shade, food and drink within walking distance

This colorful, vibrant playground is across the road from Bellevue Square. The play-lot is near a large water fountain and gathering area. A paved walkway traverses a grassy portion of the park. The tot-lot and park are popular throughout the year. Food can be found on Main Street and at Bellevue Square.

CLYDE BEACH PARK

92nd Street and Lake Washington Boulevard East, Bellevue

Access: Parking; stroller access

Features: Play equipment for tots (slides, climbers), sand play area surface, restrooms

No changing table, no food or drink available, no nursing privacy, no shade

Located on Lake Washington, small Clyde Beach Park is a place where older kids may want to swim. Toddlers will be attracted to the boat-shaped climbing structure. This "boat" is basically the entire playground, but it has enough ins and outs and ups and downs to  keep any child busy. There is a field behind the playground, but it is a little too steep for babies to enjoy.

CROSSROADS PARK

8th Street and 160th Avenue NE, Bellevue

Access: Parking; stroller access

Features: Play equipment for tots (slides, swings, climbers, bouncers), woodchip play area surface, restrooms, food and drink at Crossroads Mall, shade

No changing table, no nursing privacy

This playground, which is popular with the under-three set, is behind the Crossroads Community Center and next to a large grassy field. A paved pathway meanders through the park. There is ample shade along the grassy parkway. Restrooms and vending machines are in the community center.

See the Crossroads Community Center description, page 66.

ENATAI BEACH PARK

35th and 108th Avenue SE, Bellevue

Access: Parking; stroller access

Features: Restrooms, picnic tables, sand beach

No changing table

There is no play equipment at this park. However, it has such great beach and lawn areas that I still recommend visiting if you want to have a picnic and let your little one splash in the water.

FOREST HILL PARK

13232 SE 51st Street, Bellevue

Access: Street parking; no stroller access

Features: Play equipment for tots (slides, swings, climbers), Astroturf play area surface

No restrooms, no changing table, no food or drink available, no nursing privacy, no shade

A dirt path about the length of a high school track loops around the sunny playground at Forest Hill Park. If your stroller does well on grass, you can reach the playground with it. Because it is a couple of hundred feet from the street, you may prefer to use your stroller regardless of the difficulty. There is no shade so you'll want to keep your visit short on sunny days. This park is best to visit if you live nearby as parking is scarce.

HILLAIRE PARK

6th Street and 160th Avenue NE, Bellevue

Access: Parking; stroller access

Features: Play equipment for tots (slides, swings, climbers), woodchip play area surface, restrooms, little shade

No changing table, no food or drink available, no nursing privacy

This quiet neighborhood park is located far enough from Crossroads Mall to offer some privacy. Because it is small and unshaded, it is probably best to come here in the early morning.

IVANHOE PARK

Northup Way and 168th Avenue NE, Bellevue

Access: Parking; no stroller access

Features: Play equipment for tots (slides, swings, climbers, bouncers), woodchip play area surface, nursing privacy, shade

No restrooms, no changing table, no food or drink available

Large evergreens shade this little playground and park. On a drizzly spring day the park may seem dark, but on a hot summer day it is an ideal place to take your sun-sensitive baby. You can sit on a blanket of grass under a tree while your toddler enjoys well-shaded play equipment.

KELSEY CREEK COMMUNITY PARK AND FARM

(425)455–7688

13204 SE 8th Place, Bellevue

Farm hours: Daily 9:30 a.m.–3:30 p.m

Access: Parking; stroller access

Features: Play equipment for tots (slides, swings, climbers, bouncers), Astroturf play area surface, restrooms, food and drink in vending machines, some shade

No changing table, no nursing privacy

Kelsey Creek Park is a huge park with a colorful play area suitable for new walkers. Several grassy areas are available for sitting with younger babies. Hiking trails wind around the park, so take your child carrier to enjoy these.

Kelsey Creek Farm, which is just above the playground, is open to the public and offers children the opportunity to see farm animals up close. The farm has many activities geared toward children three years old and older. A forty-five minute farm tour may be fun for younger toddlers in addition to older children.

KILLARNEY GLEN PARK

19th Street and 104th Avenue SE, Bellevue

Access: Parking; no stroller access

Features: Play equipment for tots (slides, swings, climbers), woodchip play area surface, nursing privacy, shade

No restrooms, no changing table, no food or drink available

A charming playground, tennis courts and an open field await you in the midst of an evergreen forest at Killarney Glen Park. Hiking trails weave in and out of the wooded boundary and a sunny meadow provides a superb area for picnics. The absence of a restroom makes a lengthy visit impractical.

LAKE HILLS PARK

14th Street and 164th Avenue SE, Bellevue

Access: Parking; stroller access

Features: Play equipment for tots (slides, swings, climbers), woodchip play area surface, restrooms, some shade

No changing table, no food or drink available, no nursing privacy

This four-star park is divided into two sections: One part has an apparatus in the shape of a ship for small children to climb on; the second is filled with all types of pipes, rings and slides for climbing and swinging. A pathway leads to a bridge with slides descending into the play area. The equipment may be too advanced for your one-year-old, but the older toddlers really enjoy themselves.

LAKEMONT COMMUNITY PARK

5170 E Village Park Drive, Bellevue

Access: Parking; stroller access

Features: Play equipment for tots (slides, swings, climbers), woodchip play area surface, restrooms: Yes

No changing table, no food or drink available, no nursing privacy, no shade

Large Lakemont Community Park lies north of Village Drive, the road leading into the Lakemont development. Here, tennis courts, trails, basketball courts and a playground are available to the public. The sunny playground sports a boat-shaped play structure that is fun for toddlers, although the slide may be too high for most.

LAKEMONT HIGHLANDS PARK

15800 SE 63rd Street, Bellevue

Access: Parking; stroller access

Features: Play equipment for tots (slides, swings, climbers), Astroturf and woodchip play area surface

No restrooms, no changing table, no food or drink available

No nursing privacy, no shade

This beautifully landscaped playground is built into a small hillside. At the top of the hill are climbers, then slides that resemble a waterfall cascade down. At the bottom of the slides is another playground with swings. If the small parking lot on 63rd Street is full, you can park on 62nd Street and take the paved path to the play areas.

MEYDENBAUER BEACH PARK

419 NE 98th Avenue, Bellevue

Access: Parking; stroller access

Features: Play equipment for tots (slides, swings, climbers, bouncers), pebble play area surface, restrooms, nursing privacy, some shade

No changing table, no food or drink available

At Meydenbauer Beach Park a paved walkway leads you under Lake Washington Boulevard, connecting the parking lot to the beach and playground. It is quite a jaunt and going down is effortless, but be aware that you'll have to push your stroller or carry a tired tot all the way back up to the car. The small, sunny playground has an easy climber surrounded by rubber mats; however, the slide is a bit steep. A smidgen of beach on Lake Washington is available for digging in sand or wading; lots of grass fills in the remainder of the park.

MEDINA PARK

12th Street and 80th Avenue NE, Medina

Access: Parking; jog stroller access

Features: Play equipment for tots (slides, climbers), woodchip play area surface, restrooms, nursing privacy, some shade

No changing table, no food or drink available

Grassy slopes surrounding a quaint duck pond at this beautifully landscaped park. A gravel path loops around the rustic site. At the time of this writing, the play lot was being updated. It is a pleasant park to visit with pre-crawlers who are happy sitting still on the lush grass while you take in the scenery.

NEWPORT HILLS PARK

60th Street and 120th Avenue SE, Bellevue

Access: Parking; stroller access

Features: Play equipment for tots (swings, climbers), pebble play area surface, restrooms

No changing table, no food or drink available, no nursing privacy, no shade

If you live in the Newport Hills area and want to walk to a park, this small playground next to a playfield may be for you. However, wooden climbing structures always present a risk of splinters, especially for children under two who need to hold on to the sides. The enclosed tube slide might be scary for a young toddler.

NORTH ROSE HILL WOODLANDS PARK

9930 124th Avenue NE, Kirkland

Access: Parking at Fire Station 26 adjacent to park, stroller access

Features: Tot play structures (climbers, slides), bouncers, woodchip play surface, paved pathways, picnic areas, shade, nursing privacy

No restrooms on site, but the Fire Station restrooms are available for use (closed during a fire response), no changing tables

This park contains several tot-focused play structures: houses, a fire truck and ride-on toys. The best part is that it is all fully fenced!

ROBINSWOOD COMMUNITY PARK

24th Street and 148th Avenue SE, Bellevue

Access: Parking; stroller access

Features: Play equipment for tots (slides, swings, climbers, bouncers), woodchip play area surface, restrooms, some nursing privacy, shade

No changing table, no food or drink available

A delightful little duck pond is a short distance from the playground at Robinswood Community Park. The grassy area surrounding the pond is an ideal spot for a picnic lunch. Trees dapple the park and playground with shade. The playground provides enough excitement to keep your toddler busy and happy.

WILBURTON HILL PARK

128th Avenue and 2nd Street NE, Bellevue

Access: Parking; stroller access

Features: Play equipment for tots (slides, swings, climbers, bouncer), woodchip play area surface, restrooms, food and drink in vending machine, nursing privacy, shade

No changing table

Large Wilburton Hill Park hosts trails, tennis courts, a botanical garden and a colorful playground. Look for the playground in the park's southeast corner. Five little playhouses sport small-town names such as U.S. Post Office and General Store; climbers follow the same theme. A ladder and stairs help toddlers reach the top of the town hall. Youngsters can also climb in a wooden play ship, boat and railroad station. The restrooms and vending machines are a bit of a walk to the north.

Kirkland, Redmond & Woodinville

ANDERSON PARK

(425) 556–2300
7802 NE 168th Avenue, Redmond

Access: Parking; stroller access

Features: Play equipment for tots (slides, swings, climbers), pebble play area surface, restrooms, food and drink nearby, shade

No changing table, no nursing privacy

Located in the commercial area of Redmond, this park offers a fine resting point for picnicking and playing. A small playground adorns the southeastern tip of the park. Redmond Parks and Recreation uses quaint cottages in the park for classes.

See the Anderson Park/Redmond Parks and Recreation description, page 64–66.

CRESTWOOD PARK

6th Street and 18th Avenue, Kirkland

Access: Parking; stroller access

Features: Play equipment for tots (slides, swings, climbers, bouncers), woodchip play area surface, restrooms, limited nursing privacy, some shade

No changing table, no food or drink available

You will find the toddlers' play-lot at the northeast corner of Crestwood Park. The park also contains a number of hiking trails and a playfield. A high school uses the playfield, but the park appears big enough to accommodate everyone. There is ample parking.

EVEREST PARK

8th Street and 5th Avenue S, Kirkland

Access: Parking; stroller access

Features: Play equipment for tots (swings, climbers, bouncers), woodchip play area surface, restrooms, nursing privacy, shade

No changing table, no food or drink available

At Everest Park the play-lot lies unshaded in the middle of a large playfield. A more serene place to visit is the wooded portion of the park by the north parking lot. Here, trees lend shade to a small, quiet area bordering a narrow creek. A little bridge that crosses over the creek leads you to a path in the sunny center of the park.

FARRELL-MCWHIRTER PARK

19545 Redmond Road, Redmond

Access: Parking; stroller access

Features: Play equipment for tots (swings, climbers), sand play area surface, restrooms, nursing privacy, shade

No changing table, no food or drink available

This large park hosts a farm with pens for viewing a variety of farm animals. An expansive field is available for picnics or play. Take the trails that wind around the wooded portion of the park and stop at the play equipment down by the creek. Parking is a little distance from the farm, so you'll want to take your stroller.

FORBES CREEK PARK

116th Place and 106th Lane NE, Kirkland

Access: Parking; stroller access

Features: Play equipment for tots (slides, swings, climbers), woodchip play area surface, shade

No restrooms, no changing table, no food or drink available, no nursing privacy

If you live in the Forbes Creek neighborhood you may want to visit this park. A quiet play-lot can be a perfect place to rest on a stroller walk. Nearby on 100th Street and 117th Place is Spinney Homestead Park, which you can also take in as part of a stroll around the neighborhood.

GRASS LAWN PARK

Old Redmond Way and 148th Avenue NE, Redmond

Access: Parking; stroller access

Features: Play equipment for tots (slides, climbers, swings), pebble play area surface, restrooms, nursing privacy, shade

No changing table, no food or drink available

Over 28 acres of property make up this park with the simple name. Of the park's two playgrounds, the one near the parking off Old Redmond Way has better equipment and better shade. In addition to playgrounds, the park includes sheltered picnic tables, open fields, trails and restrooms, making it perfect for families with children of all ages.

HOUGHTON BEACH PARK

Lake Washington Boulevard and 60th Street NE, Kirkland

Access: Parking; stroller access

Features: Play equipment for tots (slides, climbers), woodchip play area surface, restrooms, food and drink, nursing privacy

No changing table, no shade

Sunshine, sand and lawn make up this waterfront park. There is little shade, so take sunscreen. The play lot is adequate for toddlers. Although the playground is located on a busy boulevard, a high fence keeps the little ones safe. Kidd Valley Hamburgers is across the street.

IDYLWOOD PARK

38th Street and West Lake Sammamish Parkway NE, Redmond

Access: Parking; stroller access

Features: Restrooms, changing table, food and drink in vending machines, nursing privacy, shade

No play equipment for tots

This park located on Lake Sammamish is a fine spot for a family outing. Not only is there a beach, but there are also woods and fields for those not interested in swimming. The parking lot is a bit far from the park, so take your stroller.

JONATHAN HARTMAN PARK

17300 NE 104th Street, Redmond

Access: Parking; stroller access

Features: Play equipment for tots (slides, swings, climbers), woodchip play area surface, restrooms, changing table, shade

No food or drink available, no nursing privacy

Jonathan Hartman Park is located next to the Redmond swimming pool and is across from Redmond High School. The park has ample shade near the playground. Ballfields that host Little League games edge the western half of the parking lot.

JUANITA BAY PARK

Forbes Creek Drive and 98th Avenue NE, Kirkland

Access: Parking; stroller access

Features: Restrooms, nursing privacy, some shade

No play equipment for tots, no changing table, no food or drink available

Come sit under the beautiful willow trees and absorb nature with your little one. Take your stroller on the paved path through this reserve on Juanita Bay. This tranquil locale should to be sought out if you love soft grass with a little shade. However, parking may be hard to find on a sunny day.

MARYMOOR PARK

6046 NE West Lake Sammamish Parkway, Redmond

Access: Parking; stroller access

Features: Play equipment for tots (slides, swings, climbers, bouncers), woodchip play area surface, restrooms, nursing privacy, shade

No changing table, no food or drink available

A large windmill and totem pole welcome visitors to fascinating Marymoor Park. The beautiful grounds of Willowmoor Farm Historic District have a wealth of things for people of all ages

to do. The Clise Mansion holds a museum of the history of the Eastside. The Marymoor Wetland Trail provides a pleasant walk through a wildlife preserve. The Marymoor Velodrome is an exciting place to watch bicycles zooming by. If all that is not enough, a large playground is available for children of all ages to romp, run and climb until exhaustion. The Sammamish River Trail, which eventually becomes the Burke-Gilman Trail and runs into Seattle, begins at the park entrance.

MEADOW PARK

106th Street and 106th Avenue NE, Redmond

Access: Parking; stroller access

Features: Play equipment for tots (slides, climbers), dirt play area surface, shade

No restrooms, no changing table, no food or drink available, no nursing privacy

This neighborhood park stands out for its well-shaded tot-lot. The playground is situated at the southwest corner of a rolling meadow. The paved pathway winds around the small park, so a summer evening stroll can easily end at the playground for some last-minute energy burn-off.

NORTH KIRKLAND PARK

124th Street and 103rd Avenue NE, Kirkland

Access: Parking; stroller access

Features: Play equipment for tots (swings, climbers, bouncers), woodchip play area surface, restrooms, changing table, nursing privacy, shade

No food or drink available

This bright, colorful playground is perfect for little acrobats. The climber's train theme gives the park its charm. Shaded grassy sections invite you to sit with your young baby. Across the street is the North Kirkland Community Center with activities for the little one. You will also find restrooms with changing tables at the center.

See the North Kirkland Community Center description, page 72–73.

PETER KIRK PARK

4th Street and Central Way NE, Kirkland

Access: Parking across the street; stroller access

Features: Play equipment for tots (slides, climbers), woodchip play area surface, restrooms, food and drink at Kirkland Park Place, some shade

No changing table, no nursing privacy

Visit Peter Kirk Park after shopping at Kirkland Park Place. The large downtown park has a playfield, benches and a playground. You can pick up some good food at Noah's Bagels or QFC Grocery and have a picnic while your little one crawls or toddles around on the grass. The Kirkland Library and Peter Kirk Pool are on the southwest corner of the park.

PHYLLIS A. NEEDY HOUGHTON PARK

10811 NE 47th Street, Kirkland

Access: Street parking; stroller access

Features: Play equipment for tots (swings, slides, climbers, bouncers), woodchip play surface, sand play area, large grassy area, restrooms, picnic tables, shade, nursing privacy

No changing table

Because it is fully fenced, this neighborhood park is the perfect place to take toddlers who are newly into exploring on their own. You can allow your child to enjoy their newfound freedom without worrying if they will run into the street. Grab lunch to go at Burgermaster on your way to the park and enjoy a fun afternoon with your child.

SPIRITBROOK PARK

6500 NE 151st Avenue, Redmond

Access: Parking; stroller access

Features: Play equipment for tots (slides, climbers, swings, bouncers), pebble play area surface

No restrooms, no changing table, no food or drink available, no nursing privacy, no shade

This quaint playground won't intimidate young toddlers with its small climber and slide. However, the little pond is quite close to the playground and could become an attractive nuisance to inquisitive youngsters.

TANGLIN RIDGE NEIGHBORHOOD PARK

NE 185th Street and 151st Avenue NE, Woodinville

Access: Parking

Features: Play equipment for tots (slides, climbers), woodchip play area surface

No restrooms, no changing table, no food or drink available, no nursing privacy, no shade

Because of its small size, I wouldn't recommend driving out

of your way to visit this park. However, if you live close by, it's a perfectly good place to let your toddler play. A bonus of a park this small is that you don't have to run all over the place to keep an eye on your child.

VAN AALST PARK

4th Street and 13th Avenue, Kirkland

Access: Parking; stroller access

Features: Play equipment for tots (slides, swings, climbers, bouncers), woodchip play area surface, little shade

No restrooms, no changing table, no food or drink available, no nursing privacy

You can't miss the fluorescent-colored climbing structure in this small triangular park. This quiet neighborhood park is fine for a walker or crawler. There is little shade for younger babies..

WAVERLY BEACH PARK

6th Street and Waverly Way W, Kirkland

Access: Parking; stroller access

Features: Restrooms, shade in morning hours

No play equipment for tots, no changing table, no food or drink available, no nursing privacy

This pretty beach park is best for babies who cannot yet crawl. Instead of a sand bank, cement steps lead down into the water. I mention this beach because it is very attractive; however, be wary of your crawler or walker getting too near the water. Large trees that border the park to the east lend morning shade.

WOODINVILLE HEIGHTS NEIGHBORHOOD PARK

NE 182nd Street and 146th Avenue NE, Woodinville

Access: Parking; stroller access

Features: Play equipment for tots(slides, climber), rubber mat play surface, picnic table, some shade

No restrooms, no nursing privacy

This small neighborhood park is a nice place for your little one to get out and stretch his or her legs if you're visiting Woodinville. It's also a great park to head to for an afternoon of play if you live in the area. Look closely in the hillside of the play area to find a hidden slide.

Newcastle, Issaquah & Renton

GENE COULON MEMORIAL BEACH PARK

1201 N Lake Washington Boulevard, Renton

Access: Parking; stroller access

Features: Play equipment for tots (slides, swings, climbers), sand play area surface, beach, restrooms, food and drink available, little nursing privacy, minimal shade

No changing table

Spread along the southeast shore of Lake Washington, this park has beaches, playground, volleyball courts and more. There is plenty of fun to be had at this popular beach park. Pull into the South Beach parking lot if you want to be near the playground, and then take your stroller for a walk to the pavilion, where you can pick up lunch at Ivar's or Kidd Valley.

KIWANIS PARK

815 NE Union Avenue, Renton

Access: Parking on 7th Avenue; stroller access on 7th Avenue

Features: Play equipment for tots (slides, swings, climbers), sand play area surface, nursing privacy, some shade

No changing table, no food or drink available

This playground sits across the street from an elementary school. The City of Renton hosts a children's after-school program in the park, so it can get busy in the late afternoon. Large evergreen trees shade a grassy area on the southeast corner, but the playground is all sun, so take sunscreen.

LAKE SAMMAMISH STATE PARK

Lake Sammamish Road and 17th Avenue NW, Issaquah

Access: Parking; stroller access

Features: Play equipment for tots (slides, climbers), sand play area surface, restrooms, food and drink, nursing privacy, shade

No changing table

This large state preserve sits at the south end of Lake Sammamish. Besides an excellent public beach, this popular eastside destination has trails, picnic tables and volleyball nets. In summertime it becomes very busy. Although there are lots of shady spots, the playground and beach are quite sunny, so take plenty of sunscreen.

MEMORIAL PARK

140 E Sunset Way, Issaquah

Access: Parking; stroller access

Features: Play equipment for tots (slides, swings, climbers, bouncers), woodchip play area surface, restrooms in the library, nursing privacy, shade

No changing table, no food or drink available

Find this playground near the library and the Issaquah Depot Museum. The clean, colorful play equipment is a popular destination for toddlers. Shade, which dapples the playground, is deeper around the picnic benches and grass. Unfortunately, the only restrooms are in the library, which isn't open until 11 a.m.

LAKE BOREN PARK

13000 SE 84th Way, Newcastle

Access: Parking; stroller access

Features: Play equipment for tots (slides, swings, climbers), woodchip play area surface, portable toilet, minimal nursing privacy

No changing table, no food or drink available, no shade

A paved walkway with ups and downs loops around Lake Boren Park, making it a great place for running with a stroller. Newer playground equipment is suitable for toddlers but the lack of shade makes sunscreen a must. A grassy field is perfect for romping and rolling.

LIBERTY PARK

Bronson Way N and Houser Way N, Renton

Access: Parking; stroller access

Features: Play equipment for tots (slides, swings, climbers, bouncers), woodchip play area surface, restrooms, nursing privacy, some shade

No changing table, no food or drink available

This large park is sandwiched between I–405 and Maple Valley Road, making it a bit noisy. The playground sports a large climbing structure.in A sunny field is available for running and romping or having a picnic. There are also plenty of picnic tables. Located next to the Renton Public Library, this park makes a nice side trip after a library outing.

NEWCASTLE BEACH

4400 SE Lake Washington Boulevard, Newcastle

Access: Parking; stroller access

Features: Play equipment for tots (slides, swings, bouncers), woodchip play area surface, restrooms, nursing privacy, some shade, vending machines for drinks

No changing table (there is a bench in the restroom), no food available

This 29-acre park is located on Lake Washington. Shaded picnic benches next to the small sunny playground are close enough for you to sit while watching your toddler play. The train in the play area is perfect for smaller children. The swimming beach lets little ones stick their feet in the cold water. If grassy fields are more your style, there is an open area for picnic blankets and relaxing.

THOMAS TEASDALE PARK

601 S 23rd, Renton

Access: Parking; stroller access

Features: Play equipment for tots (slides, climbers), sand play area surface, restrooms, food and drink available, nursing privacy, minimal shade

No changing table

The playground at Thomas Teasdale Park is better for older children because the climbers may be difficult for small children to use. However, there is plenty of grass to run around on and picnic tables in shelters if it rains.

Bothell, Edmonds, Lynnwood, & Mill Creek

BRACKETT'S LANDING NORTH (EDMONDS UNDERWATER PARK)

Main Street and Railroad Avenue, Edmonds

Access: Parking; stroller access

Features: Restrooms, beach access, picnic area, food and drink nearby

No changing table, no shade

North of the ferry landing, this park is well known for its ideal teaching environment for scuba divers

because of its shallow waters and abundant underwater sea life. It's also a great place to bring your child for exploring the beach. There's lots of driftwood and shells along the sand and rock beach, and sometimes you can find a crab under a rock. The seagulls are not timid here, so be cautious if you decide to have a snack.

BRACKETT'S LANDING SOUTH

Main Street and Railroad Avenue, Edmonds

Access: Parking; stroller access

Features: Picnic area, grassy area, food and drink nearby

No restrooms, no changing table, no shade

South of the ferry landing, this park is mostly sand beach. If your child loves to wade in the water, this part of Brackett's Landing is much less rocky and better for new walkers. This area also has a large grassy area for your child to play on, as well as paved pathways for walking. If you're hungry, walk south to Arnie's Beach Café. They have outdoor seating and are accommodating to those with children.

BLYTH PARK

16950 W Riverside Drive, Bothell

Access: Parking; stroller access

Features: Two play structures for tots (slides, climbers, wood bridge, swings), sit-on sand diggers, woodchip play surface (slides land on rubber mat surfaces), tires embedded in ground to climb on, restrooms, picnic tables (covered and uncovered), shade, nursing privacy

No changing table, no food and drink available

Cross a small bridge and drive down what seems to be a country road to Blyth Park. Situated above a river, this park is open, yet private at the same time. This is likely a result of well laid out picnic and play areas. There is a lot of space for your child to run around, and the tire structures are a unique addition that will certainly help build climbing coordination.

CITY PARK

3rd Avenue South and Howell Way, Edmonds

Access: Parking; stroller access

Features: Play equipment for tots(climbers, slides, swings), woodchip play surface, wading pool, picnic tables, restrooms, nursing privacy, food and drink nearby

No changing table

Nestled on the edge of downtown Edmonds, this park is a haven for parents and children. The wading pool, close to the entrance of the park, is fully fenced, making it much easier to keep an eye on your toddler. There are covered picnic tables and lots of trees for shade. The play equipment is divided into two areas, one for older children and one for the youngsters. The area designated for the littler children has lower climbing equipment, tot swings and bouncers. This play area is in direct sun so be sure to slather on the sunscreen when you visit.

COUGAR PARK

3475 148th Street Southeast, Mill Creek

Access: Street parking; stroller access

Features: Play equipment for tots (climbers, slides), climbing structure and rock wall for older children, sit-in spinner, woodchip play surfaces, restrooms, covered picnic structure

No changing table, no nursing privacy, no food and drink available

Located across the street from Mill Creek Elementary, this 5-acre neighborhood park was recently upgraded. There are no tot swings; however, the tot structure is great for toddlers because it's lower to the ground and has a short slide. The climbing structure and rock wall are definitely aimed at older children.

DALEWAY PARK

190th Street Southwest and 64th Avenue West, Lynnwood

Access: Parking; stroller access

Features: Play equipment for tots (swings, slides, climbers), summer spray area, picnic facilities, restrooms

No changing table, no food and drink available

More than half of this park is forested, so despite being fairly near busy Highway 99, you'll feel like you're far from the city. The summer spray area is open from June through November and operates at the push of a button for 15 minutes; from 11 a.m. to 6:00 pm. This park is popular with local childcare centers in the summer, so be prepared to keep a close eye on your toddler while older children play.

FAIRBANK FARM

(425) 743-3694 www.fairbankfarm.com

15308 52nd Avenue West, Lynnwood

Hours and fees: Saturday and Sundays in October 10 a.m.–5 p.m.; $2.50 per person

Access: Parking; stroller access

Features: Portable restroom and hand washing station

No changing table, no nursing privacy

Although the Fairbank Farm may only be open to the public in October, it's worth the wait. When you visit, your admission

fee includes seeing (and petting) chicks, ducklings, calves, sheep, goats, ponies, pigs and rabbits! The farm provides a cup of animal food to each visitor. This is great way for your child to learn about farm life and see animals up close, something not always possible at the zoo. Pumpkins are available for sale also.

LYNNDALE PARK

189th Street Southwest and 72nd Avenue West, Lynnwood

Access: Parking; stroller access

Features: Play equipment for tots (climbers, swings, slides), woodchip play surface, asphalt park trails, soft surface hiking trails, picnic tables, restrooms, nursing privacy

No changing table, no food and drink available

Lynndale Park is a 40-acre community park just north of Lynndale Elementary School. Home to the Pacific Little League, this park also has a soccer field, tennis and basketball courts and a skate park. This park is laid out very well. The play area is away from the athletic fields and courts, so you can visit without worrying about your little one being run over by the big kids. The trails are also great if you want to take a stroll.

MARINA BEACH

Admiral Way South, Edmonds

Access: Parking; stroller access

Features: Play equipment for tots (climbers, slides), woodchip play surface, picnic tables, restrooms, paved pathway, beach access, some shade, grass lawn area, food and drink nearby

No changing table

I might never have expected this park to be kid friendly, had I not picked up an "Exploring Edmonds Parks" brochure at the community center and noticed a picture of a play structure right next to a beach! The play structure is about 50 feet from the beach and is enclosed by a short retaining wall. This wonderful waterfront park also has a smooth sand beach with lots of shells and driftwood, perfect for your young explorer, especially at low tide.

MEADOWDALE NEIGHBORHOOD PARK

5700 168th Street Southwest, Lynnwood

Access: Parking; stroller access

Features: Play equipment for tots (slides, climbers), wood structure with slide and tunnel, woodchip play surface, sand play area, swings, paved trail, picnic tables, grassy meadow, shade, nursing privacy, restrooms

No changing table, no food and drink

Most of this park is preserved forested space. If you're visiting with your infant, you can walk the paved or nature trails. The tot play gym and sand area will keep your toddler busy. If you have older children, the 60-foot cable swing will make them happy to hang out at the park, too.

NORTH LYNNWOOD NEIGHBOORHOOD PARK

185th Street Southwest and 44th Avenue West, Lynnwood

Access: Parking; stroller access

Features: Summer spray pool, play equipment for tots (climbers, slides), , restrooms, picnic shelters, large grass play areas, asphalt loop trails, nursing privacy, food and drink nearby

No changing table

If you drive by too quickly, you'll miss the entrance to this park, located next to Lynnwood Elementary. The park is back

from the road and is marked by a small sign that blends in a bit with the landscaping. After you've found it, this is a fantastic park for your little one. The summer spray pool has water that sprays up from spigots in the ground and also from a large dragon's head above. The sprays are fairly gentle and good for tots still working on their balance. The park is quite large and has plenty of space to spread out and play or just relax. The parking lot is fairly small, so if the lot is full, and you're not visiting during school hours, park in the school's parking lot and walk across their grounds to the park.

PINE MEADOW PARK

15803 32nd Avenue SE, Bothell

Access: Street parking; stroller access

Features: Play equipment for tots (climbers, slides), grassy play area, covered picnic area, restrooms, short paved trail, nursing privacy, shade

No changing table, no food and drink

This park is located in an upscale neighborhood in Mill Creek and is surrounded by beautiful homes. This park is very well manicured and clean. There is lots of room to spread out and enjoy playtime.

PINE STREET PARK

A Avenue and Pine Street, Edmonds

Access: Parking

Features: Play equipment for tots (swings, climbers, slides), woodchip play surface

No restrooms, no changing table, no nursing privacy, no shade, no food and drink available

This small neighborhood park in Edmonds may not have the amenities that the larger parks in the Edmonds area have. Nevertheless, the park is well maintained and worth visiting if you live in the area and are looking for a small, less crowded park to take your child to play.

SAINT EDWARD STATE PARK

14445 Juanita Drive NE, Kenmore

Access: Parking; stroller access

Features: Tot play area (play airplane, house, sand pit, riding toys), play equipment for tots (slides, climbers), mock ferry, woodchip play surface, picnic tables, shade, restrooms, nursing privacy

No changing table

This 316-acre state park juts up against 3000 feet of shoreline along Lake Washington. There is no direct access to the water–you must take a trail to get there. What is especially attractive about this park is that the tot area is fully fenced. The large castle play structure will keep experienced walkers and older children entertained for quite some time.

SPRUCE PARK

168th Street Southwest and 36th Avenue West, Lynnwood

Access: Parking; stroller access

Features: Summer spray pool, tot-lot (slides and spinning blocks), woodchip play surface, asphalt loop trail, forest trail, picnic areas, restrooms, nursing privacy

No changing table

This is a well-shaded, quiet, neighborhood park. It's easy to get to and has plenty of parking. The play area is back from the road and is great for your new walker or toddler with its large, wide slide. There is a trail that loops around the park if you feel like taking a walk while you're there.

WILCOX PARK

52nd and 196th Street Southwest, Lynnwood

Access: Parking; stroller access

Features: Play equipment for tots (slides, climbers, swings), woodchip play surface, sand play area, restrooms, shade, nursing privacy, picnic tables, food and drink nearby

No changing tables

Wilcox Park is adjacent to busy 196th Street Southwest and is considered to be a neighborhood park. However, because the park is so big, it feels much more spacious than a typical neighborhood park. There is a large grassy area and lots of trees. There are two play structures, one for younger children, and one for older children, so even on busy days, there is plenty of room for lots of youngsters to play.

Notes

Shopping

Grocery Store Playrooms

Some grocery stores in the Seattle area offer free childcare within the store, in a playroom filled with toys and activities. Usually your child must be over two, but does not have to be potty-trained. If your child has a soiled diaper or starts to cry, the staff will page you over the intercom. Don't count on your baby cooperating every time, especially around the age when separation anxiety kicks in. If your child is eager, it is a wonderful way to handle grocery shopping. The following locations offer childcare:

FRED MEYER

(206) 297-4300
915 NW 45th St Ballard

(425) 865–8560
2041 NE 148th Street, Bellevue

(206) 433–6411
14300 S First Avenue South, Seattle

(425) 235–5350
17801 SE 108th Avenue, Renton

(425) 416-1100
6100 E Lake Sammamish Parkway, Issaquah

(425) 670-0200
4614 196th Street SW, Lynnwood

(425) 566-8000
17667 NE 76th Street, Redmond

QFC–UNIVERSITY VILLAGE

(206) 523-5160
2746 NE 45th Avenue, Seattle

Shopping Malls

Shopping malls are excellent spots to take your baby when the weather is poor. From newborn to two years old, a young child loves the stimulation of people, colorful lights and the attractive window displays. Also, parents enjoy being among other adults while entertaining their young one at the same time. My son has always enjoyed going to the mall. Even at seventeen months he remained content just to ride in the stroller while I window-shopped.

Overall, Nordstrom has the best nursing areas of all the stores. They usually provide a quiet room with comfortable couches and low lights. Changing tables are permanent fixtures, not the plastic pull-down type, which I never feel at ease using. Macy's comes in a close second, but the rooms were not as private or cozy as at Nordstrom. J.C. Penney and Sears usually have plastic pull-down changing tables and there is no place to nurse comfortably. The best nursing area or changing table at the mall is noted first.

Under the food category I have concentrated on places that offered baby-friendly foods, although there may be other places in the mall to eat.

ALDERWOOD MALL

www.alderwoodmall.com

184th Street and Alderwood Mall Boulevard SW, Lynnwood

Children's Apparel: The Disney Store, GapKids, Gymboree, Janie & Jack, J.C. Penney, Macy's, Nordstrom, Sears, Stride Rite

Toys: Build-A-Bear Workshop, The Disney Store, Liam's Toy Box

Food: Claim Jumper, Jamba Juice, McGrath's Fish House, Nordstrom Café, P.F. Chang's, Ramano's Macaroni Grill, Ruby's Diner, The Terrace Food Court

Play area: Yes, near Sears

Restrooms and changing tables: Nordstrom's ladies lounge is on the second floor on the side opposite the elevator. J.C. Penney's is on the first floor by Customer Service. Macy's is on the mall level by the elevator and on the second floor by the elevator. Mall restrooms are in the food court.

Nursing privacy: Nordstrom's ladies lounge has an area for nursing. There is a semi-private area within the restrooms located in The Terrace Food Court.

Alderwood Mall is a large shopping complex in Lynnwood. The majority of the mall is indoors, but the outdoor addition allows you to enjoy time outside during your shopping trip. The play area is great for toddlers, with soft climbing toys and wall activities. It can get quite crowded, which sometimes can be overwhelming for younger children. Target and Toys 'R Us are just on the outskirts of the mall and are also excellent for baby necessities.

BELLEVUE SQUARE

www.bellevuesquare.com

8th Street and Bellevue Way NE, Bellevue

Children's apparel: The Children's Place, GapKids, Gymboree, Janie & Jack, J.C. Penney, JoJo Kids, Macy's, Nordstrom, Oilily, Sears, Stride Rite, Talbot's Kids

Toys: Build-A-Bear Workshop, Learning Quest Toys, LEGO, Pottery Barn Kids, The Right Start

Food: Auntie Annie's Pretzels, The Cheesecake Factory, McDonalds,

Nordstrom Café, Orange Julius, PF Chang's, Pagliacci Pizza, Red Robin, Taco Del Mar, World Wrapps, Z'Tejas Southwestern Grill

Play area: First level, East Common, in front of Eddie Bauer; second level, East Common, near J.C. Penney

Restrooms and changing tables: Nordstrom's ladies lounge is on the second floor on the side opposite the elevator. J.C. Penney's is on the first floor by Customer Service. Macy's is on the mall level by the elevator and on the second floor by the elevator. Bellevue Square's "family restrooms" are on the first and second level by Nordstrom.

Nursing privacy: Nordstrom's ladies lounge has an area for nursing. Macy's women's restroom on the mall level has chairs for nursing.

Bellevue Square is the crème de la crème of malls in the Seattle area. It has the standard department stores as well as every chain store that offers children's items. The one downside to this two-story shopping complex is the lack of convenient elevators. Only one elevator is located in the middle of the mall; another is to the west by the exit. Each department store has its own elevator as well, so use them when you find them. One of the best children's stores in Bellevue Square is The Right Start. It's a great source for interesting baby accessories, and you can avoid the shipping charges you'd pay through the catalog.

CROSSROADS MALL

www.crossroadsbellevue.com

8th Street and 156th Avenue NE, Bellevue Children's apparel: Kid's Club, Old Navy

Toys: Kids Club, Uncle's Games

Food: Chili's, Guido's Pizzeria and Wine Bar, Firenze Ristorante Italiano, and the food court "Public Market Eateries"

Play area: Coin-operated carousel

Restrooms and changing tables: Mall restrooms by Old Navy

Nursing privacy: None

The large food court is the central attraction of this mall. While you get a bite to eat, you little one will be entertained by watching the people eating at the multitude of tables that fill the center of the mall. You can find something for the most finicky eater from the wide selection of food. Old Navy, one of the few stores that carr clothing for babies at this mall, is noted for high quality, inexpensive clothes. Check out the socks—they do not slip off tiny feet and have little rubber traction grips on the soles.

FACTORIA MALL

www.factoriamall.com

36th Street and 128th Avenue SE, Bellevue

Children's apparel: Mervyns, Nordstrom Rack, Old Navy, Osh Kosh B'Gosh

Toys: Rite Aid, Target

Food: Burger King, Flavor Bakery and Café, Jamba Juice, Orange Julius Grill, Red Robin, Torero's Mexican Restaurant

Play Area: The KidsQuest Children's Museum is located inside Factoria Mall between Mervyn's and Old Navy. The museum has engaging activities for all ages, from newborn to age 12. The exhibits incorporate science, art, technology and daily life, with a focus on the Pacific Northwest. KidsQuest Children's Museum is open Tuesday, Wednesday, Thursday and Saturday 10 a.m.–5 p.m., Friday 10 a.m. –8 p.m, and Sunday 12 p.m.–5 p.m. Fees: Children under one free; all others $6; Friday evenings from 5 p.m.–8 p.m. are free for everyone.

Restrooms and changing tables: Factoria Mall's women's restroom near Pearl Vision has a counter; Target also has a changing table in their restroom

Nursing privacy: Women's restroom in the mall near Pearl Vision

This small mall is located in southeast Bellevue. Mervyn's and Target have a great selection of reasonably priced children's clothing and shoes. If you want to avoid big mall crowds, this is a fine place to shop. The KidsQuest Children's Museum will make it even more attractive to your child.

GILMAN VILLAGE

www.gilmanvillage.com

317 NW Gilman Blvd, Issaquah

Children's apparel: Boys Only, Spoiled By Nana

Toys: Lilypad Books, White Horse Toys

Food: Bamiyan Afghan Cuisine, Bangalore–Cuisine of India, Boarding House Restaurant, Nicolino Ristorante Italiano, Tantalus Greek Bistro

Play area: none

Restrooms and changing tables: In mall restrooms

Nursing privacy: No

This quaint outdoor mall consists of historic homes and cottages renovated to into stores and restaurants. Brick sidewalks and wood decking give the mall the feel of an old Northwest town. In addition to the shops listed above, there are interesting gift and jewelry stores that are fun to explore. Check out the color displays at the candy store Sweet Additions, but be prepared for a lot of "I want's" from your toddler.

LAKE FOREST PARK TOWNE CENTRE

17171 NE Bothell Way, Lake Forest Park

Children's apparel: none

Food: Food court adjacent to Third Place Books in upper level

Toys: Rite Aid, Third Place Books (book related)

Play area: In Third Place Books

Restrooms and changing tables: In Third Place Books restrooms

Nursing privacy: Yes, in children's section and couches in food court

On the second floor of the Lake Forest Park Towne Centre is Third Place Books, a wonderful bookstore. The bookstore offers new and used books and provides a children's section in the southeast corner. Soft beanbag chairs in the middle of this section

offer another comfortable nursing area that will work well if you have an older child in tow. While you feed the baby, your other child can read books or play with blocks provided in baskets on the floor near you. Also on the second floor near Third Place Books is a large food court. The food court has enough variety to please any palate. Along with tables and chairs, couches are available for semi-private nursing.

NORTHGATE MALL

www.simon.com

Northgate Way and 5th Avenue NE, North Seattle

Children's apparel: Gap, Gottschalks, Gymboree, J.C. Penney, Macy's, Nordstrom, Payless Shoe Source, Toys "R" Us

Toys: EB Games, Toys "R" Us

Food: Auntie Annie's Pretzels, Azteca, California Pizza Kitchen, Red Robin, and a food court

Play area: None

Restrooms and changing tables: Nordstrom second floor by Town Square; J.C. Penney first floor by lingerie; Macy's ground floor level by the lingerie department and second floor by the linen department, food court

Nursing privacy: Nordstrom ladies lounge has an area for nursing; Macy's women's lounge is on the second floor.

Northgate Mall was the very first shopping mall in the country, after which others in the U.S. were patterned. It is smaller than Bellevue Square and Southcenter, but still has most of what one expects to find in this type of shopping complex. Northgate Mall is in the process of expanding, and over one million square feet of shopping is planned. The Red Robin restaurant is very child friendly and has lots to look at which will keep your toddler occupied.

REDMOND TOWN CENTER

www.redmondtowncenter.com

Leary Way and 76th Avenue, Redmond

Children's apparel: Brat Pack, GapKids, Gymboree, Macy's

Toys: Brat Pack, EB Games, Learning Quest Toy's, Uncle's Games

Food: Claim Jumper, Cucina! Cucina! Italian Café, Desert Fire Southwestern Grill, Pizza Schmizza, Red Robin, Ruby's Diner and many others

Play area: Yes, between Ruby's Diner and Gene Juarez

Restrooms and changing tables: In mall restrooms on north side, ground level

Nursing privacy: No

This outdoor mall offers two levels of shops and restaurants. A cover over the aisles of shops provides rain protection. A street runs through the center of the mall, so watch your toddlers. Near the Starbucks is an active water fountain in which your kids can play. There is plenty of covered parking.

SOUTHCENTER MALL

Southcenter Parkway and Tukwila Parkway, Tukwila www.westfield. com/southcenter

Children's apparel: Abercrombie Kids, Children's Place, GapKids, Gymboree, J.C. Penney, Macy's, Mervyn's, Nordstrom, Payless Shoe Source, Sears

Toys: Character Corner, K-B Toys

Food: Bahama Breeze, Olive Garden, Rainforest Café, and a food court

Restrooms and changing tables: Nordstrom ladies' lounge and men's room third floor and second floor; J.C. Penney second floor; Macy's second floor; Sears second floor; Mall restrooms in the food court

Nursing privacy: Nordstrom's ladies' lounge third floor has a pleasant nursing area; Macy's ladies' lounge also has a nice area for nursing.

Southcenter Mall is a large shopping mall in an even larger

shopping district just south of Seattle. Most of the chain retail stores have a spot here at Southcenter or along the outskirts of the mall.

UNIVERSITY VILLAGE

45th Street and 25th Avenue NE, Laurelhurst

Children's apparel: Gap Kids, Kid's Club, Pottery Barn Kids, Sole Food, Village Maternity

Food: Delfino's Pizza, Jamba Juice, Johnny Rockets, QFC, Ram, World Wrapps, Zao Noodle House

Toys: Bartell Drugs, Kid's Club, Land of Nod, Pottery Barn Kids

Play area: A remodeled play area with a play structure is outside, near Nine West and Fireworks Gallery

Restrooms and changing tables: The University Village restrooms, and Barnes and Noble

Nursing privacy: None

University Village is an excellent place to come for most of your shopping needs. It is an outside mall, so come prepared in inclement weather. There is enough cover over the promenade that you will not need an umbrella, although the Village has complimentary ones placed around the center. The play area in the middle  of the mall is a fine place for your toddler to let off steam before going into another store. Life-sized sculptures of a cow and calf, which always attract youngsters, pay homage to the time when this property was part of a Carnation milk-bottling plant. In front of the Ram Restaurant is a stone water sculpture that children can play in, although it may be a bit much for toddlers.

QFC has a childcare room available for children over two. Barnes and Noble bookstore alone is worth the trip to University Village. This huge store has a wonderful selection of children's books and has storytime several times per week.

Just north of the University Village on Blakely Street, which turns into Union Bay Place, you'll find the Right Start, Pinocchio Toys, and All for Kids.

Notes

Quick Reference Guide

Creepers, Crawlers & Toddlers INSIDE

Creepers, Crawlers & Toddlers OUTSIDE

Newcastle, Issaquah & Renton

Bothell, Edmonds, Lynnwood, & Mill Creek

Shopping

Grocery Store Playrooms

Shopping Malls

Index

Other Books by JASI

The Best of Central California: Main Roads and Side Trips

Bob Carter

Award-winning writer Bob Carter covers everything from missions to wineries along highways 1, 101, 99, 395, and 14. Includes trips off the beaten path.

$14.95, 303 pages, ISBN 1881409104

The Best of Orange County California: A Guide to Scenic, Recreational and Historical Attractions • Second edition

Gregory Lee

This guidebook includes restaurants, beaches, museums, well-known theme parks and lesser-known recreational gems.

$16.95, 304 pages, ISBN 1881409260

The Brewpub Explorer of the Pacific Northwest • Second edition

Hudson Dodd, Matthew Latterell and Ina Zucker

This fully updated edition is the perfect companion to help readers explore the multitude of micro-breweries in Washington, Oregon and British Columbia.

$16.95, 256 pages, ISBN 1881409252

California's Gold Rush Country: A Guide to the Best of the Mother Lode

Barbara Braasch

From assay offices to tailing wheels and antique fairs to wine tours, this book is packed with travel tips and "don't miss" attractions for all seasons.

$14.95, 203 pages, ISBN 1881409147

Discover Washington with Kids
Third edition

Rosanne Cohn & Larry Kahn

Updated version of this popular family guide to Washington State tells where to go with kids in tow. Explores well-known landmarks, hidden treasures, and great adventures.

$16.95, 272 pages, ISBN 1881409295

Other Books by JASI

Discover the Southwest with Kids

Mary Vasudeva

From ancient Indian cities to frontier forts, from national parks to museums, festivals and magical out-of-the way places, this is an indispensable guide.

$16.95, 256 pages, ISBN 1881409244

Breakfast in Seattle, 2nd Edition

Kay Vail-Hayden and Marilyn Dahl Gjording

Revised edition of this one-of-a-kind popular guide to the first meal of the day. The authors provide culinary ratings for a meal that is rarely covered by the restaurant reviewers.

$14.95, 208 pp, ISBN: 1881409317

Las Vegas on the Dime: An Insider's Guide to Great Values

Michael Toole

This something-for-everyone guide tells visitors and locals where to find the best buys in everything from souvenirs to shrimp cocktails to CDs.

$14.95, 208 pages, ISBN 1881409279

The Essential San Juan Islands Guide
Third edition

Marge and Ted Mueller

This new edition covers dining, lodging, shopping, boating, bicycling, camping, and special festivals.

$16.95, 304 pages, ISBN 1881409287

The Pitiful Gardener's Handbook: Successful Gardening in Spite of Yourself

Connie Eden & Tracy Cheney

This easy to understand handbook will appeal to anyone looking to make the right time- and money-saving decisions to achieve happy gardening results.

$12.95, 176 pages, ISBN 1881409236

Other Books by JASI

Oregon's Coast: A Guide to the Best Family Attractions from Astoria to Brookings

Carolyn & David Gabbe

Contains information on beachcombing, dune buggy riding, tidepooling, and whalewatching.

$11.95, 192 pages, ISBN 1881409007

The Seattle Super Shopper: The Savvy Shopper's Guide to the Greater Puget Sound Area • Ninth edition

Mac and Rebecca Johnston

The latest and greatest revised best-seller of information on over 1,500 Puget Sound area places selling brand-names at rock-bottom prices.

$16.95, 256 pages, ISBN 1881409309

Spokane: The Complete Guide to the Hub of the Island Northwest

M.E. Buckham

This extensive guide to the Lilac City tells where to stay, shop, eat and play in and around this region.

$14.95, 256 pages, ISBN 1881409139

About the Author

Rebecca Johnston is a full-time mother, as well as a part-time publisher and author. Prior to taking on these roles, she worked for a local insurance company where she was challenged to develop skills in financial services, claims, litigation, sales and management. However, the real challenge came when her son Benjamin was nine months old and she decided to stay at home with him full-time.

Already inspired by Julia Rader Detering's first edition of Bringing out Baby, Rebecca jumped at the chance to revise the book when the opportunity came shortly after leaving her job. She knew this work would help to ease her into her new role and provide outings to keep Benjamin entertained and stimulated.

Rebecca enjoys making scrapbooks, traveling, reading, getting to know other moms, and exploring different activities with her son. She lives in Edmonds with her husband, son and two cats.